Improving
Newswriting

The best of The Bulletin of the
American Society of Newspaper Editors

Edited by
Loren Ghiglione

To Jessica and Laura

Contents

Editing the writer

Sportswriting

Writings on writing

Introduction

Is good writing a newsroom frill?

Loren Ghiglione

The reporter, as readers of tough-guy mysteries know, is a divorced boozer, dangling cigarette and snap-brim fedora at the ready, who joyfully lies, bribes and steals to get the story. He lives to report, not write. He writes, he'll tell you out of the side of his mouth, only to see something of his in print other than his fingers.

Reporting, that's what matters. Reporters afflict the comfortable and comfort the afflicted. Reporters win Pulitzers, achieve Woodstein-style celeb status and have themselves immortalized ("two parts bastard and one part angel") in books with titles like *The Typewriter Guerrillas*.

Why hasn't writing — good writing — counted (at least until recently) in newsrooms? Pick your theory. First, editors are an especially obtuse class of troglodyte who actively discourage good writing; copy editors let pass only the five W's and cliches. "Worst of all," H. L. Mencken once said about the plight of the reporter, "he must write stuff that will commend itself to his immediate superiors, the copyreaders — men chosen, more often than not, because they are efficient rubber stamps rather than because they are competent judges of English style." Reporters like that theory.

The second hypothesis: Journalism puts such a premium on speed — on describing complicated subjects clearly but quickly — that newspapers have no room for good writing.

Even world-class writers, who could be expected to argue for the wordsmith, come away from newspapers appreciating the importance of the reporter who can write as fast as his Remington's keys move. When Ernest Hemingway reported for the Kansas City Star, the staffer he most respected was Leonard Calhoun Moise who "could carry four stories in his head and go to the telephone and take a fifth and then write all five at full speed to catch an edition." Hemingway understood newspapers' priorities. Moise, he wrote, "was the fastest man on a typewriter I ever knew. . . .He was always the highest paid man on every paper he worked on."

A third theory pictures journalism as a kind of training activity, similar to learning to type, from which young people one day ascend, like a late repentant rising from the second terrace of Dante's purgatory, to a higher craft, writing. Lillian Ross, in the introduction to the 1981 edition of *Reporting*, warns, "If you are on the staff of a newspaper and if what you want is to become a writer, don't stay on the staff for more than two or three years."

Whatever the explanation, good writing has been relegated for years to newspapers' broom closets, on the top shelf, next to the rolls of toilet paper. Editors blame the American educational system. Less emphasis on writing and reading, they argue, has led to a generation that specializes in ungrammatical, graceless prose.

One study of American high schools concluded that "careful writing has apparently gone about out of style." In 17 years, from 1963 to 1980, verbal Scholastic Aptitude Test scores dropped almost 12 percent.

But newspapers also have been part of the problem. They have cared about reporting. About all the news that's fit to print. About the first rough draft of history. But they haven't cared about how rough, how unpoetic, that draft is.

For a half century, writing was noticeably absent from the convention programs of the American Society of Newspaper Editors and from the pages of the Society's magazine, The Bulletin. Those articles that did appear focused on word usage. Edward J. Meeman, editor of the Memphis Press-Scimitar, argued tongue in cheek for the formation of SPIREL, the Society for the Preservation, Improvement and Restoration of the English Language. Rebecca Gross, editor of the Lock Haven (Pa.) Express, philosophized on the use of Mr., Mrs. and Miss (the world, in 1962, had not yet discovered Ms.).

In the mid-1970's, editors began to worry about writing. Aware that newspaper circulation was lagging behind population growth, they started to fret over how newspapers could compete with the visual fireworks of television. One possibility: four-color writing to create striking word pictures in readers' minds. "The more colorful, dynamic and stimulating the writing," a Gannett study noted, "the more satisfied the reader becomes."

So newspapers hired writing coaches to work with reporters. Editors attended writing seminars. Papers appointed assistant managing editors whose primary responsibility was to overcome the second half of Oscar Wilde's line about the difference between literature and journalism: "Literature is not read and journalism is unreadable."

In 1976, Tim Hays, editor and co-publisher of the Press-Enterprise, Riverside, Calif., and a past president of ASNE, proposed that the Society draw attention to the importance of good writing. Editors, Hays said, "are neglecting a job we supposedly are best equipped to handle. That is, improving writing in our papers. If we can't do that, we might as well quit."

In 1978, under President Gene Patterson, editor of the St. Petersburg Times, the Society offered a convention session on writing and began sponsoring an annual Writing Awards Contest. First directed by Tom Winship, editor of The Boston Globe, and then by David Laventhol, publisher of Newsday, the contest now attracts almost 700 entries annually in four categories: deadline writing, nondeadline writing, commentary and sports.

The Modern Media Institute, which coordinates the writing contest, publishes the winners' stories for ASNE in an annual volume, *Best Newspaper Writing*. Roy Peter Clark, the director of MMI's writing seminars, edits the book, supplementing the stories with interviews of the winners about the writing process.

ASNE also emphasizes the importance of writing through expanded Bulletin coverage. This book, drawn from two decades of Bulletin issues, relies most heavily on special reports on writing that have appeared at least twice a year since 1979.

One question remains. Will newspapers' current emphasis on good writing survive? Unsuccessful attempts at good writing — sentences overstuffed with similes and metaphors — could cause a reaction, a return to just-the-facts-ma'am prose. Editors could view good writing as only another fad, one of journalism's hoola hoops, undeserving of continued support.

I'm not good at crystal gazing. Each year I pick the Red Sox to win the American League pennant. But my money is on the survival of the writing movement. It will endure. It must.

LOREN GHIGLIONE, editor and publisher of The News, Southbridge, Mass., was editorial board chairman of the ASNE Bulletin from April 1980 to April 1982.

Newswriting

Writing is an art, not a craft

James Kilpatrick

The thought occurs to me from time to time that newspapermen too seldom think of themselves as writers. They are, if you please, reporters, or critics, or specialists in labor news; they are sports columnists, food editors, book reviewers or editors of editorial pages. They cover politics. They are assigned to the courts. They are observers. They are members of a staff. In the flatulese that passes for English, they are even "communicators."

But what do they do for a living? They *write*. They put words together — written words — to convey thought. And in the end, the test of how well they do their job is not how well they edit, cover, observe, review or criticize, but how well they write.

That is what I propose to discuss — a few notes on the writing art. My reason is largely personal: I know enough of myself, after all these years, to know that I am not a notably deep thinker, nor an especially accurate prophet, nor a remarkably erudite scholar.

Whatever skills I may have as a newspaperman are chiefly the skills of a writer. This is how I have earned my living, with my belly against an Underwood, for almost 30 years. Most of the millions of words I have put together in this time, as Dr. Douglas Southall Freeman used to say, have been written on sand, or on the wind. No matter. I believe I may have learned something of the tools of a writer's trade; so I pass these thoughts along.

Forgive me if I speed by the guidelines to "clear" writing. Students, especially, will have heard the lecture on "clear" writing a dozen times; and if the outer limits of your journalistic ambition lie in communicating no more than yesterday's stationhouse blotter: "Fortescue Ipswich, 64, was arrested on Tuesday on a charge of stealing the archbishop's cassock" — perhaps a few such lectures will suffice.

My thought was rather to turn around on the broader theme of "effective" writing. There's a difference. The poetry of Kazantzakis is marvelously effective, but it is not always clear.

Some of the fundraising editorials we write may be clear, but they may not prove effective.

Most of us, if we love writing, and spend our lives at the task, want to write at a level higher than the troubles of Fortescue Ipswich. If our aim is to amuse, to inform, to persuade, to arouse, to delight, we want to do an effective job of amusing, informing, persuading, arousing or delighting. We have gone beyond the creditable ambition to write clearly; we aspire to write gracefully or literately, or wittily, or perceptively. How do we go about it?

The short answer, I suppose, is that God alone knows. By this I mean to suggest that good writing — the kind of writing I am talking about — is an art, not a craft; and there is truth in the melancholy thought that craftsmen are made, but artists are born. The phrase that ignites a sentence, and leaves an incandescent glow behind, is fused from within.

But I think a good deal can be done to make the spark more effective. In my own observation, the best writing I encounter is the work of writers who have trained themselves to look intently, to listen carefully and to read voraciously.

By "looking intently," I have in mind the kind of looking described by the little girl in Lee Smith's beautiful first novel. She proposed "to look very carefully at a thing, so it would stay in my mind forever."

In the last few weeks, a good many editorial writers, obedient to hallowed tradition, tried their hands at editorials intended to herald the arrival of spring. A few of these change-of-pace pieces were markedly better than the bulk of them, and for this reason: They were the work of men who looked intently at spring, and did not fake it, or rely on recollection, or simply string together a few pretty words.

If you propose to write about the advent of spring, to write effectively about it, you must go to the countryside and look at spring intently: How does a twig grow? How does a bud swell? How does the green leaf uncurl? Is the leaf green? What tint or shade of green? Consider the dogwood blossom, how it grows, the promise of drowsy summer in its chalice. One must smell the earth, put his hands in it, marvel at the tangle of roots and leaves and humus.

It is this intentness that produces the images, similes, metaphors. If we look in this fashion, we may describe how a flower *really* is. Our writing will ring true. And when we then select judiciously from all that is recorded by the camera eye, pulling out the significant details, we make a start toward effective writing.

Do you remember Lawrence Durrell's description in *Clea* of an air raid by night on Alexandria? He saw the searchlights "stalk about the sky, quivering and sliding, like daddy-long-legs." The exploding rockets "emptied their brilliant clusters of stars and diamonds and smashed pearl snuff-boxes." He remarked "the greasy buttocks of the barrage balloons." He saw at last what the searchlights were seeking: "six tiny silver moths, moving down the skylanes with what seemed unbearable slowness."

Durrell, you see, had looked intently at an air raid. But you will object: Durrell is a novelist, and writing novels is one thing, but reporting is another. Very well. In 1946, Rebecca West covered the Nuremberg trials. She sat in the courtroom, as other reporters did, but her gift was to look intently. Thus she saw the defendant Streicher: "He was a dirty old man of the sort that gives trouble in parks." She saw the defendant Schacht: "He became stiffer than ever, stiff as an iron stag in the garden of an old house." She covered those trials not only as a reporter, but also as a writer; and her writing endures. Two decades after Nuremberg, we read Rebecca West, and we see Nuremberg as it was.

If we look intently, and listen carefully, and read voraciously, in time we begin to discover how the good writer works. We discover the importance of cadence; we learn that a sentence simply "sounds better" — sounds better to the inner ear — if the accented syllables fall into ordered arrangement. We learn to see in similes, to see the thing itself and the thing it looks like: searchlights and daddy-long-legs, stiff Prussians and iron stags.

My grandmother, so far as I know, never wrote a line for publication, but she had some of the instincts of a writer: She saved everything. She was forever putting boxes in the attic — scraps of lace, bits of cloth, rubber bands, crochet hooks, jar tops. What was the point of it? "It might come in handy some day," she would say; and she would label another shoe box.

I have a notion that if a man would write well — write beyond the level of Fortescue Ipswich — he must create a grandmother's attic: He must collect words, phrases, images; he must collect colors; scents, sounds, movements, textures; he must cultivate an acute perception of the commonplace: the flat tire, the burned-out bulb, the broken lace, the missed note, the third strike, the queasy sensation that strikes a man when he perceives he has run out of gas. It is just as grandmother said. A Romney quits in New Hampshire; a Reagan fails in Miami. We have stored the bits and pieces, knowing they might come in handy some day.

What I am saying, I suppose, is that our task as writers is eternally to translate the particular event in terms of the universal experience. When we succeed, we lance through a reader's inattention with the blaze of a watchman's torch. We read such a line and say, "Ah. That's how it is; that's *exactly* how it is."

Such writing, I scarcely need to remark, is both agony and ecstasy. Mostly agony. Over a long period of years, I used to write upwards of 20,000 words a week for publication. Most of it was the archbishop's cassock, to be sure, but some of this output aimed a little higher. And I used to long for one good sentence — just one good sentence a week. Lord, I would pray, let me fashion today one good sentence only, and every night of my life I will light candles of thanksgiving. I still begin each day at the desk with that prayer; and out of rueful recognition of the countless times it has gone unanswered, I commend it, fellow sinners, to you.

JAMES J. KILPATRICK, formerly editor of the Richmond News Leader, has been writing a syndicated column full-time for 15 years. This article, published in the June 1969 Bulletin, was adapted from a talk before the Georgia Press Institute.

The hard work of writing better

Paul Swensson

I agreed to try to tell how to turn out a beautiful piece of vivid writing and how to report with mirror-like simplicity. And now the deadline crumples my mind.

Why do I fear putting down the first line? Can't I make up my mind what to say?

And why can't I see you, the reader, any better than yesterday when I could not tell the color of your eyes or hear the sound of your words on paper as you sit at your typewriter and I at mine.

I know why. I do not want to admit that when it comes to writing, we are very much alike. For your sake, don't be like me. Because I procrastinate. I find detours on the eight-foot journey from the door to my desk. I am greedy and impulsive, grasping clusters of words when one would do. My mind is impatient, darting like a polliwog in a pond to other attractions. I cater to my habits, both good and bad. I am insecure. I sicken when my writing is criticized. I crave encouragement and curse the postman when acceptance letters do not arrive by return mail. I suspect that my writing ills are chronic. But I live for praise from my peers and for those rare moments when one word, or phrase, or short sentence breaks out of my mind to sing gloriously.

If you accept parts of that fat paragraph as plausible images of your work habits, then we have nailed down the most troublesome problems that editors have with reporters and writers. You and I are so wrapped up in our hopes, or fears, or subject matter, that we don't, won't and can't identify the person(s) for whom we write.

If you see a blob of faces as you look up from your typewriter, stop writing. Focus on one reader. Write directly to that person. Some young writers tell me they write for just one person —their editor. That's the wrong reader.

Tons of research have been printed and a mint has been spent to identify audiences. We know much about demographics of our readers and every bit helps. But we rarely discover how we turn off readers, one by one. Readership research explores the one-to-one relationship. One writer. One reader. If you, the writer, see your reader clearly, you are one-third of the way toward serving and satisfying that reader.

It matters not greatly whether you have picked a bright or dull reader, a lazy one or one in a hurry, a young one or an old one, a him or a her; but it must be a real person. Your editor may suggest that you change the reader just as you change subject matter. But you need a reader, one for whom you are a servant.

John Steinbeck said it well when he sat down to write *East of Eden* for his two small sons. "Perhaps by speaking directly to them, I shall speak directly to other people." Later he said: "One can go off into fanciness if one writes to a huge, nebulous group."

What can a writer expect of a reader? What do I expect from this conversation with you?

I want you to be curious and skeptical, but not cynical.

I hope that our eyes will meet and that your head will nod in approval a few times. I expect to see your dissent with a frown and negative shake of the head. I hope that between nods, shakes and frowns you will give me your attention to the end of this piece.

Two things I must do for you. I must write clearly, so that you are not confused. I must share something of value with you, lest you turn the page and leave without a farewell.

The late Gideon Seymour made a habit of substituting a Greek-rooted word for every Latin word in his first draft of editorials for The Minneapolis Star. The Greek words he wanted had powers of persuasion; the Latin words were good but limited to precision. He wanted to persuade. Therefore he swapped syllables until he found the combination that would work for him. You can swap words, too, and you need not be a Latin or Greek student to do it well. But it helps.

Walter Kerr marshaled words of sight and sound to describe a dance in "No, No, Nanette": "The boy's shoes are cleated beneath those diamond-patterned socks, and as the fast-tap begins, the stage floor flinches. It is jackhammer time . . . ." Even the "diamond-patterned socks" suggest speed and the image of motion.

Listen to the sound of words from Hemingway's *The Sun Also Rises:*

"They had hitched the mules to the dead bull and then the whips cracked, the men ran, and the mules, straining forward, their legs pushing, broke into a gallop, and the bull, one horn up, his head on its side, swept a swath smoothly across the sand and out the red gate."

Look at that sentence. Count the verbs, adverbs and adverbial phrases which bring together the facts of place and thing and set them in rapid motion.

Between the inertness of the dead bull (he is merely hitched) and the smooth speed with which the body sweeps across the sand and out of sight are verbs of sweat and effort: crack, run, strain, break. Precisely at "broke" the sentence stops straining and moves into the smooth glide to its close.

Look at the s's and the th's of swath smoothly. These are not inadvertent. They ease the path of the bull's departure and are marks of Hemingway's skill in using the sound of words.

Norman Cousins, the editor and publisher, hunts for persons who use words well in writing about the arts, or politics, or science or about some remote corner of human experience. Cousins says of this kind of writer:

"Whoever and wherever he is, he likes the clink and purr of words against each other. He likes the crackle of ideas well expressed. He delights, as some men do in thoroughbred horses and racing hulls, in prose that runs sleek and true to its destination."

James Kilpatrick, the columnist, adds this caution: "With a little rearranging you can keep the rhythm going. But do not do this always; you may sound like Hiawatha."

Choosing the right word is a game anyone can play. A Washington sports announcer, having delivered Chris Hamburger to the Redskins training field one week after emergency appendectomy, said Hamburger would not play for two weeks lest "he reinjure" his stomach muscles. The announcer was wrong twice with one word. Hamburger had never injured his stomach muscles. Therefore he could not reinjure that which had not been hurt, unless the surgeon's scalpel counts as an injury.

Jerry Lewis, according to Hub Keavy, an Associated Press writer, reads papers for material in his night club acts. "What," he asked a member of the audience, "is a woman's 'yet' "? After a pause Jerry says, "I don't know either, but here's what I read in the paper: 'The prowler shot the woman and the bullet is in her yet.' "

Let's detour around the right word to let strong words beat sense into our erratic habits. A plaque in the Milwaukee Press Club says: "The ability to express ideas is as important as the ability to have ideas." That's where the strong words come in.

Weather stories depend on the selection of words with muscles. Paul Montgomery wrote in The New York Times: "Punishing winds and driving snow lashed the Northeast yesterday, producing heavy snow accumulations inland and perilous conditions along the coast."

The lead could be faulted for vagueness about the storm, but it uses powerful words to identify the impact on people. If you wish, underline *punishing* and *driving, heavy* and *perilous*. These are words, not meteorological vocabulary.

You may be tempted to remind me that much of your writing deals with technical matters. You feel committed to dullness because of the subject matter. If you really think along those lines, you are digging a grave for your writing. Dullness can be overcome. Here is a method, in the form of a quiz, that works for me.

Here are five kinds of news stories: *things, ideas, people, projects, problems.* Rank them in the order you think will get the most reader attention. Put in the No. 1 slot the most interesting type of story. Then list the others down to No. 5 in descending interest.

Researchers confirm that readers are interested above all in what happens to other people. *People*-oriented stories earn the No. 1 rank. Second are *things* which are triggered by man or nature. Third are the *project* stories where something useful is supposed to happen. Fourth, *problems*. Fifth, *ideas* which usually require an extra effort to appreciate or understand.

If you are assigned to write about a problem, research it for its human qualities and write it in terms of a real person with a real problem. Do not generalize.

Never write about the Irish problem, the Arab problem, the Israeli problem, the Black problem, the Indian problem or the Ms. problem. Turn it the other way around: then write.

Alliteration can be used to step up the impact of strong words. A Time magazine writer described how the Thad Jones musicians "blow, beat or belt their way into a piece." Shakespeare played with the impact of words in *Midsummer Night's Dream* when Puck recites: "I'll lead you about a round, Through bog, through bush, through brake, through brier; Sometime a horse I'll be, sometime a hound, a hog, a headless bear, sometime a fire, And neigh, and bark, and grunt, and roar and burn Like horse, hound, hog, bear, fire, at every turn."

Whether you accept the tip from Shakespeare or Time, the words you use in common writing can be put in two piles — the strong words and the soft or weak words.

Blow, beat and belt from Time, when spoken aloud, are expelled from the throat, they sail between parted teeth and get their final shape from the lips. Puck used strong words 21 times in the passage above.

Soft words also are shaped in the throat; they float up with little effort and out with lips barely parted. Often they are not heard at all. But they provide mood.

Some words shout, others sigh. Make them work for you.

Somehow I missed the real reason for reading Chaucer in school days. He was the greatest among English poets for the use of language as an effective instrument of action. Rexroth says Chaucer used language to get results. He steers readers to 15 lines in the "Prologue" where Chaucer defines mercantile capitalism with the skill and understanding of a Marx, and with considerably fewer words.

When shaping a sentence or rewriting a paragraph, scrutinize the hardness or the softness of the essential words. Add or subtract the decibels or sound as needed. Read the passage aloud, or at least whisper. This is one way to put muscle into your writing.

Newspaper writing is edging tentatively toward the broad horizons of the essay and away from the narrow scope of the five W's.

Ken Ringle tried it this way in The Washington Post: "You can see it best from somewhere atop the Continental Divide: the chilling skyscape of winter coming; the gray quilted snowclouds of late November and early December."

Except for proper nouns, he uses no word longer than two syllables to show what he wants us to see. He goes on: "They pour through the passes (usually from the west) on a silent, cutting wind and funnel out through the lonely Rocky Mountain ridges onto the barren landscape of a waiting America."

With simple words he sends your fingers to button the collar against wind and cold. Now for the third paragraph, 26 words long, in which Ringle provides title, theme and outline for his piece: "Winter is being born, and with it what Melville called the 'dampy drizzly November in my soul'; an annual late autumn crisis of life and doubt."

I had not realized until recently how far and fast some writers are running in their search for a different kind of lead paragraph. A few of the entries in the 1976 Virginia Press Women's contest were deep into the seventh paragraph before striking the chord on which they would build a melody of words. I suggested then (and now) that three paragraphs ought to be the outer limit, because readers (we can't escape them) are lazy. They must be lured with the opening words, such as Ringle's "you can see it best ..."

But before your next words hop to their perches on the typewriter carriage, please check your clothesline. This piece of rope, on which you hang your literary wash, is also known as the outline. I prefer to call it clothesline because I can look at what I have hung on the line and I can see if all the (verbal) socks are up and matched. I can also see the empty place saved for the shirt of an idea that somehow isn't there.

Jacques Barzun in *Simple and Direct* nails down the importance of logic to writing, if one is to say exactly what one wants to say: "Language is not algebra ... the symbols do not stay put, nor can they be carried from place to place with an assurance that their value will not change. If language were like algebra, there could be no poetry or other fiction, no diplomacy or intimate correspondence, no persuasion or religious literature."

As soon as your lead or theme is set, the next goal must be the last paragraph. That's where you want to take the reader. The last part may take many forms, but most often it affirms the lead. The writer has not done his/her job well until the reader says: "I'm glad I read all of this. Now I understand what I had not grasped before."

Or even better, the reader may be moved (as you wanted him/her to move) to do something positive on a course of action. Or the reader may give silent thanks to the author of the good words. Grace before and after a meal of words is not a silly thought.

Only the better writers make a habit of starting and finishing each paragraph with an interlocking stitch, the thread which ties ideas together at the same moment it ties the idea to the reader.

You can trust your editor in the role of word surgeon who ties syllables with surgical knots so the thoughts cannot slip away. That's part of the shared labor between writer and editor. But sometimes the editor can only point out passages where passages are not passages. In the margin or in a cover note words appear: "It doesn't hang together."

The reason may be found in one of several traps. It could be departure from the outline or the natural arrangement of the subject matter. Or it could be fouled in the beginnings or endings of difficult sentences or paragraphs. Or it could be in the selection of words, or the omission or insertion of direct quotations. Barzun, like others, avoids dogmatic prescriptions to achieve "linking" in one's writing so that "clusters of untrimmed thought" are connected in the best order. He recommends watching how good writers do it, then learning from them.

How does a person turn out "a beautiful piece of vivid writing" or report with "mirror-like simplicity"? Much can be learned about the correct or acceptable use of English. Strunk and White's *The Elements of Style* is still the best for many of us. Why be grammatical? Simply to insure a safe journey of words from one mind to another. Why fight jargon? For the same reason that environmentalists battle pollution.

Fine writers are born, not made. But every writer, regardless of the gift that is his or hers, must learn to use simple words, must battle adjectives and adverbs, must discover the right word and must realize how well words work in short combinations.

Every writer must find in solitude the rhythms which swing thought into speech ... and learn without being taught the movement and counter-movement of words to move the action down the page to the story's end. But for every fine plan and procedure there are worms and waste — physical, mental, emotional and spiritual — the aches and agues a writer is susceptible to.

At 75, Carl Sandburg said: "If God gives me five more years," he (Sandburg) might become a writer.

John Steinbeck in a letter to his editor wrote: "Sometimes I have felt that I held fire in my hands and spread a page with shining — (but) I have never lost the weight of clumsiness, of ignorance, of aching inability."

If you ache enough you may be well down (or up) the road to becoming a writer.

PAUL SWENSSON, former newspaperman, Newspaper Fund director and journalism professor, is a newspaper consultant. This article, published in the April 1978 Bulletin, originally appeared in Matrix magazine.

Creative writing in the newsroom

Everett Allen

In January 1966, at the suggestion of my editor, I began writing a Sunday editorial-page column entitled The Present Tense. I chose the title because I wanted something that would cover everything, assuming that, in due course, I would wish to write about everything. The Present Tense suggests this concept to me: We are, we remember, we hope, so that, in a sort of devious way, the words which delineate what the column intends cover not only the present, but the past and future as well, allowing the subject to go whichever way it chooses.

Five of these columns published in 1978 were awarded in May the American Society of Newspaper Editors' writing award in the commentary category, as well as the ASNE's first annual Editors' Award, thus providing for me this opportunity to address a subject dear to me, the role of creative writing in American journalism.

I am well aware that many, including both academicians and editors, would tend to be skeptical concerning the existence of any such role. I once was acquainted with a publisher who deplored what he referred to as "personal journalism," that is, any effort to bring one's personal style into the writing of a newspaper story. He was strictly a who, when, where, what man — a good newspaperman — who nevertheless felt that it was unprofessional, for example, for an interviewer to write so well that the style in a certain sense competed with the subject of the interview.

I am also conscious, from personal experience, of the practical inhibitions facing a creative writer in the newsroom: lack of time, lack of space and, often enough, lack of encouragement from editors in various capacities. However, nobody ever said that applying creative writing to journalism's demands was the easiest way of earning your money — but if anybody really wants to write, rather than simply hitting the keys of a typewriter, he will find a way to do it.

In this connection, it may be of documentary interest that my first Present Tense column was published ten years after I submitted the samples initially. In the meantime, two, and perhaps three editors had changed their minds as to whether it was worth publishing. I have written these pieces for 13 years and have never done one of them on company time; there is no such time available to me for this kind of thing, nor any atmosphere in which the necessary related reflection can be accomplished. I write them at home, on Sunday mornings. As for space, they appear on the editorial page, because there simply isn't any other place to put them.

However, having said all this, I still stand firm in the notion that creative writing can be accomplished during the working day and as an integral part of day-to-day stories that are published in the news columns. One can still do it and make his deadlines; learning to write well rapidly is no easier and no harder than any other worthwhile discipline. What it amounts to is whether you are willing to rebel professionally against writing the first lead and the first phrase that come to mind — the ones that almost everyone else has chosen since journalism became a fact.

There are, of course, some hard truths. People in American newsrooms — any newsrooms, one assumes — are divided into at least three categories: those who cannot write but nevertheless fulfill the requirements of accuracy and clarity; those who probably could write, but never will because they do not have to, and those who possess some writing ability, or at least the writing urge, and who undergo daily frustration because they do not find an adequate outlet for it.

Persistence is the thing, for those in the latter category.

Over the years, I have reveled in such indulgences in news stories as (a) quoting from Anacharsis' "Diogenes Laertes" (written about 600 B.C.) in the story of a New Bedford fishing vessel missing for ten days in a bad blow. The quote was, "On learning that the sides of a ship were four fingers thick, he concluded the passengers are just that distance from death," and (b) when geologist John Chase found a piece of tektite on Martha's Vineyard — some suggest tektite may be a chunk of the moon — I was moved to note what scientific advances, including moon landings, have done to the centuries-old romantic concepts of that satellite.

I observed, "No, Virginia, there is no man in the moon, nor is the moon a goddess any longer. We know, for we have stepped into the moon's boudoir and observed it naked, and do you know what it is? It is a pitted, dead gray expanse that rejects life and love, an old and empty place whose monotonous items we shall now subject to a cataloguing so exhaustive that there will remain no lunar corner where doubt or mythology, or green cheese, or romance, or Santa Claus can lurk.

"My father, Joseph Chase Allen, once wrote, 'When the moon walks upon the water,' in recalling those years when he went down to the sea in ships. I am not even sure that he would dare write that line now, for fear that he would get a terse postcard from NASA ground control in Houston informing him: 'The moon really does not walk upon the water. This is an illusion.' "

I once used a Latin phrase in a waterfront story — it was about a fellow who had overcome severe difficulties, a really good yarn of courage and hard work paying off, and I wrote "ad astra per aspera," which is to say, "to the stars through hardships." My editor flayed me for it, beginning with a scornful note that asked: "For the benefit of our Latin readers?" I pointed out to him that most of our fishermen at that time were Roman Catholics and churchgoers and that they were exposed to Latin at least once a week. I observed that the particular phrase is the motto of Kansas, which, for all I know, may have fewer residents exposed to Latin in a given week than does Massachusetts. He was not impressed.

I add with haste here that I do not strain to use unusual phrases or large words simply for the sake of doing so, but I do not duck either if, to my mind, they are precisely what is called for. I have never written down to the readership. Everybody has two vocabularies: the one he can use and the one he can understand; I do believe that, over the years, through a maze of stories about fires, shipwrecks, antiballistic missiles, oceanography and U.N. Security Council debates, I have had a reasonable number of the readers with me most of the time. Besides, I think part of a newspaper's job is to inject a constant uplift effort. Good writing never hurt any reader, and why should stories be patterned to match the latest educational attainment level of the community if it is low?

Yet I am first of all concerned with the desire to communicate effectively. In so doing, I endeavor not to get between the reader and the subject, but rather, through the use of appropriate words and phrases, laid somewhat layer upon layer, to build a total picture for him through the use of large and small pieces. I have great affection for effective and highly selective detail. I am forever mindful of the opportunity to transmit large truths through small incidents — and having done so, do not belabor the point; I prefer to grant the reader common sense.

Here is a fragment of an interview with the engineer of a fishing trawler: "(He) invited me to take tea in his engine room, squeezed sideways against the sheathing, feet braced to avoid falling into the flying rods, and cheeks pink from the heat, because the engine took all the room there was. Thus balanced against the interminable pitch and thrash of the English Channel's crooked water, we yelled amiably at each other over the swish-ka-pow, swish-ka-pow of the jewel-like engine."

This is from a piece focused on one sea duck, aimed at supporting legislation to regulate the pumping of ship bilges offshore, because of the adverse effect upon sea birds. The duck in question had been well-tarred; we squirted gin down her throat, scrubbed her with kerosene, hot water and yellow laundry soap, and bedded her down in a backyard rabbit house, unused.

"I did not sleep that night. Several times, I went to the bedroom window, squinting futilely into the deep shadows, where Ida (the duck) waged the battle that each of us must fight essentially alone. There was no sound, no movement; nothing but interminable silence. I thought of her dead, one, big, funny foot outstretched awkwardly and her soft head unmoving on the wooden floor of the house and I could neither stand the image nor put it out of mind.

"At daybreak, I ran out, bracing myself.

"Behold, she stood, the wild sea rover. Her eyes were like jewels in the fresh morning. Feet apart, chest out and bill high, she made one demand of me — and I knew what it was. I shucked and hand-fed her a pint of quahaugs, joyous at the arrogance of her reborn appetite, unmindful of the fact that she nipped me unmercifully and unintentionally."

And this excerpt is from the story of a fire in a small place, specifically, in Boston's Chinatown, not far from Harrison Avenue:

"Now here is the late-winter shape of the crooked street; the faded letters of the battered red-and-white sign slung over the sidewalk read 'Wai Wai.' The time is 10:30 in the morning, the dirty, three-inch ice is black in the gutters and two blocks away, bright billboard bulbs announce that it is 19 above.

"This is a tight province of tumbled contrast, wall jumbled against wall, and suddenly one dreary display window blackens like a lamp chimney when the wick is too high. There is a quick, breathless puff as the glass shatters and black smoke, like a wild, thick rope, pours upward through the jagged hole.

"A woman, old enough to be my mother and agile enough to be my daughter, shiny black hair in a tight pug, comes running out of the burning building carrying a bent snow shovel, and with the fear and agony of all time in her face."

So much for the presentation of evidence.

Every reporter isn't a creative writer, but there ought to be at least one with the potential on every newspaper staff. Every story doesn't lend itself to creative writing, but there ought to be someone on every newspaper who recognizes such a story when it comes along and who can do something about it — who can create a piece that is an invitation to the reader not simply because of what it says, but also because of the manner in which it says it.

In behalf of creative writing in journalism, I rest my case at this point. But I hope that those of you who read this, who are in such an excellent position to do so, will continue to plead that case and to do everything that you can — personally and professionally — to place new and greater emphasis upon the quality of writing in your newspapers.

EVERETT S. ALLEN, editorial page editor of the New Bedford (Mass.) Standard-Times before his recent retirement, wrote this article for the July/August 1979 Bulletin.

Good writing makes the difference

Everett Allen

Cooper Gaw, a splendid, white-haired gentleman, graduate of Harvard and a constant respecter of proper English, was my mentor when I first started writing editorials. On that first day, he said to me gently, "Mr. Allen, for a while, until you learn the ropes, *I* will write about the follies of the city council and other such earthshaking matters that concern us. You will write the anemones."

Anemones? I puzzled over the word somewhat and looked it up in the dictionary. That wasn't much help. It said, regarding anemones, "of a crowfoot family, having lobed or divided leaves and showy flowers without petals, but with conspicuous, often colored sepals."

I went back to Mr. Gaw to ask him what "anemone" editorials were, in his view. He sat there, a grand old man, looking out the fifth floor window at the sparkling blue water of the harbor. He cleaned his glasses with a piece of Kleenex and he said, very thoughtfully — as if he knew that I had been to the dictionary — "Did you read that part about showy flowers without petals?"

I said I had.

"Well," he said, "every editorial page ought to have some editorials on it that are just good to read. They may not have petals — that is, perhaps they take no stand on the pressing and terrible issues of our times, but they add light, color, spirit. They are 'showy' in the better sense of that word; they invite readers who may not even be particularly interested in the subject because of the manner in which they are written and the tone that they convey. They may produce a chuckle, a tear, they may move people in the way that one is moved by a clear fall day or the face of a child. Most importantly, they leave the reader feeling that he or she could relate to whoever wrote the editorial. Such writing makes newspapers and their editorial writers seem human; newspapers ought to work at that because if they do not seem human, they cannot do their job."

I wrote anemone editorials, the first one being about a fellow who was wounded in a Greek border war that no one ever heard of who sold hot dogs from a rolling cart on our waterfront, who lived in one room, but who gave $5 to the Community Chest.

I know now, after all these years, how fundamental Mr. Gaw's point was when he said that newspapers ought to work at seeming to be human, rather than oracular. At the moment, we of the Fourth Estate would be more loved and, what is more important, better understood, if a greater number of our readers felt that we were indeed quite like other mortals. It is worth thinking about that one of the most popular editorial-page pieces I ever wrote concerned a spring morning when I fell down a manhole while walking to work.

Now I do not think the readership generally wished me ill (there may have been exceptions) but I believe basically that the readers were simply reassured to learn that someone who wrote editorials for a newspaper could, in fact, fall down a manhole just like an ordinary human being.

I have persisted in attempting to introduce creative writing into the news and editorial-page columns whenever possible and, in these latter years, this has meant encouraging others to do likewise. Over the years, as a sort of personal and private trademark, I have dropped iambic lines into stories and editorials many times, under many circumstances. Why iambic? Because the iambic is the heartbeat of the English language; more often than not, both our written and spoken words fall into this rhythm. This is, of course, easily accomplished; consider the following iambic lines:

1. (*City government*): "The mayor cast the lone dissenting vote."

2. (*Hurricane survivors looking for the missing in a city morgue*): "Today, the grateful living viewed the dead."

3. (*A sudden storm, combining hail, rain, snow and thunder*): "Last night, the weather of four seasons struck at once."

So much for gimmickry. It has served principally as a reminder to me; I have played this private little game of iambics to remind myself constantly that good writing and journalism are not, in fact, worlds apart and to prod myself into providing, as often as I could, the kind of better writing that a given situation or a given editorial may not have demanded, but did, in fact, invite.

I have always believed that if you want to write not only well, but well and effectively, you have to think, first of all, before you put a word on paper, who the reader is. If newspapers are, in fact, going to be human — if they are going to laugh, cry and sing like everybody else, if they are going to be, in fact, of, by and for the people, they have to figure out who the people are.

This business of stressing better writing in newspaper editorials goes far beyond giving additional pleasure to the reader and greater satisfaction to the writer, although it ought to do both of those, too. One of our basic weaknesses is that we accept as fact that some kinds of news and issues are dull. This is particularly true of government matters at any level, despite the tremendous amount of time, energy and space that we devote to them. We say, "There was a heated exchange in the council meeting," rather than using the quotes that made it heated. And whenever we do this kind of thing, we are ignoring the drama, the comedy, the human conflict and the fascinating insights into the operations of levers of power that are the very heart of government.

Consider these excerpts, totally different in their approach, yet both written by Pulitzer Prize-winning editorial writers — the first by Buddy Davis of the Gainesville (Fla.) Sun and the second by Ed Yoder of the once-Washington Star — and both examples demonstrating good interesting editorial writing about the government:

Here's Davis (he is protesting a Treasury Department ruling in 1950 that defined American oil company payments to oil producers abroad as tax credits, rather than plain business deductions):

"When somebody caught the late W.C. Fields examining the Bible, the bulbous-nosed comic claimed he was looking for loopholes.

"In that regard, old big nose was an amateur. Grit your grinders and peer down the Grand Canyon which the multinational oil industry bulldozed through U.S. tax laws."

He gets down to facts and figures thereafter, but I submit that is an opener that's a grabber.

Here's another early paragraph by Davis explaining how it was that the oil companies felt the need to find some kind of government relief:

"As the sheiks smartened up around 1950, they demanded more than a token share of the wealth drained from beneath their sands. Pandemonium reigned around the polished tables in the oil board rooms. And where to turn except to the benevolent great godfather who dwells in Washington Swamp?" Washington Swamp, incidentally, is what Buddy always calls the national government.

Now here is Ed Yoder. As thoughtful, articulate reasoning is beautiful, he writes beautifully. This editorial is called "The Marble Cake," and I suggest even the title invites one to read:

"For some faint-hearted people, it is a shocking aspect of the Reagan counter-revolution that the new President entertains views about the federal-state relationship that were, until lately, quite out of fashion along the Potomac."

In other excerpts, he goes on to say: "To speak of the states as 'sovereign' without the vital addendum 'within their constitutional sphere' is to wave banners that are now as tattered as bright. It was to convert a federation into a 'more perfect union' that the founders met in 1787, and whatever 'sovereignty' survived that conversion lost its ultimate meaning in early July 1863, the week of Gettysburg and Vicksburg.

"Federalism today is not a layer cake but a marble cake, with federal and state functions inextricably commingled ... it is largely a waste of time to bog the discussion down in boundary surveying when the needs are really of another sort.

"An atmosphere of partnership, the chief need, implies comity, understanding, forbearance, cooperation, mutual respect — the graces that have tended to vanish from the federal balance during some 50 years when power and revenue sources have flowed relentlessly toward Washington."

That is good, clear, thoughtful writing about a heavy government subject: I like it, all the way from such phrases as "banners that are now as tattered as bright" to the civilized, good-natured call of "the graces that have tended to vanish from the federal balance."

Government doesn't have to be dull. Writing about it doesn't have to be a dull job. And the editorial product doesn't have to be dull, either. Good writing makes the difference.

Theodore Bernstein of The New York Times, as you know, an outstanding authority on good and careful writing, said once that people generally, including people who write for newspapers, are accustomed to thinking of their everyday writing efforts as if they were forms in which one merely fills in the blanks. This is disastrous. There is always sufficient scope for originality, adroit phrasing, just as there is always the need for logical thinking and clear expression — and these are the bare bones of good writing.

Most people should not write as they talk, because they talk neither directly nor beautifully. I confess that ever since I was small, I have talked aloud to myself when alone. In talking to myself, I begin with the creation of an imaginary situation that is dramatic (a Walter Mitty sort of thing, I suppose), and that always demands that I find the best possible words, and very rapidly, in order to talk my way out of it.

This is a splendid exercise; over the years, it has improved the speed with which I can formulate a sentence that pleases me structurally and says what I want it to. In short, accepting the soundness of Mr. Bernstein's thesis on talking and writing — which this is — I have for a long time endeavored to think and talk as I write; the closer you can come to this, the easier it is to write because you are, in effect, relieving yourself of the burden of "bilingualism" and the necessity of transposing or translating from one to the other.

Accepting the effectiveness of certain idioms, colloquialisms and picturesque speech on occasion, and usually when used in quotation marks, I am nevertheless no advocate of the common usage theory as it applies to the use of the language in writing. I submit the fact that Harry Truman and Dwight Eisenhower (as you see, I am nonpartisan and objective) — that neither knew the difference between "like" and "as," a fallibility they shared with several million Americans, is no argument for suggesting that there isn't any difference. However, in defense of colorful language, even ungrammatical, I *was* moved to quote an up-country farmer in an editorial, when he said of his land, "They's a good deal more rocks into it than bread puddin' has raisins."

In striving for good writing, don't forget Will Strunk's Rule 13: "Omit needless words." Dr. Strunk stressed that: "Vigorous writing is concise. A sentence should contain no unnecessary words, a paragraph no unnecessary sentences, for the same reason that a drawing should have no unnecessary lines and a machine no unnecessary parts. This requires not that the writer make all his sentences short or that he avoid all detail and treat his subjects only in outline but that *every word tell*."

To which I add, the American verb as it is commonly used, is probably the flabbiest piece of language in the world. Consider the verb "walk." We use it as if everyone, walking along a sidewalk, looked like everyone else doing the same thing. A walk is very likely as distinguishing as a nose. Most people don't walk; they prance, mince, hobble, stride, lope, stroll, ramble or perambulate, but walk? Not often, and if you do not use the verb "walk" except when it actually *is* the best verb, then it, too, will come to mean something.

As an experiment designed to strengthen your verbs, try denying yourself adjectives and adverbs. This is akin to an art student's discipline, in which he or she must paint with a limited palette. As a simple example, it is easy enough to say, with reference to penmanship, "His writing was poor" or "He wrote poorly," but it is stronger by far to say, "He scrawled," the image thus conveyed being more vivid.

I am a great believer in the use of effective detail and an appeal to the senses, as well as to the mind. In writing, I attempt to build, layer upon layer, as if holding the subject of the piece aloft, turning it slowly so that the reader will be exposed to all aspects of it. If, in order to understand the matter in totality, this means providing the reader with sounds, smells, tastes, colors, feelings, facts, quotations, metaphors and contrasts, so be it. So long as it neither distorts nor deviates, a device that enhances communication is justified.

It is not merely aesthetic or playing games to alternate sentence lengths, to employ conjunctions, to experiment with the use of compound and complex sentences but, rather, these are ways of whetting reader interest, of taking into consideration reader interest span, of acknowledging the value of proper pacing in your writing, keeping the flow going. I am not a grammatical lint-picker and so I do not rule out, for example, the incomplete sentence. However, I remind you that Picasso did not reject perspective until he had mastered it. If you are going to use an incomplete sentence on occasion for certain effect, do be sure that you are aware it is an incomplete sentence.

As editorials do not have to be written in dull fashion, neither do they have to be written in deadly fashion. In retrospect, I believe that too many of my editorials over the years were written with a terrible iron seriousness that depressed even some of my most enthusiastic followers. Do let me offer you some excerpts of editorials on nongovernment subjects that I hope may serve to reacquaint you — we all have a tendency to forget in the day-to-day rush — with the fact that there are lots of things about which editorials may be written; lots of them offer an opportunity for a special kind of good writing, and both you and your readers need them. They provide perspective, change of pace, a new tone, and are sometimes even fun to write and to read.

Humor: "These oncoming generations with uncut thatches and unshaven beards are missing a rite which for many a decade amounted almost to an initiation into manhood. We refer to all those bottles standing in front of the mirror in any barber shop, ready to the barber's hand and in full view of the sheeted occupant of the barber's chair. What boy did not look forward to the time when he could enter the shop alone, armed at last with authority and responsibility, and at the proper moment request a dousing with Zepp's, or Herpicide, or Bay Rum, or Witch Hazel? Best of all with Lucky Tiger."

Nature: "Bountiful rain, bringing about a bountiful supply of organic material in woodland solution, has led to an unusual number of Indian pipes this summer. These white, waxy plants may be mistaken for fungi, though there's no resemblance to toadstools; the difficulty is that there's no resemblance to green plants either, for Indian pipes are parasitic, drinking up nourishment from decaying leaf mold and the like instead of relying on sunshine and chlorophyll.

"A poet once wrote of Indian pipes as a 'spotless sisterhood' and added, 'No Angelus, except the wild bird's lay, wakes these forest nuns, yet, night and day, their heads are bent, as if in prayerful mood.' "

A campaign: This is a description of a courthouse, the basis of an editorial argument in favor of building a new one: "In the first instance, this building, because of its age, limitations and general dreariness, is depressing; it is an aesthetic, personal and professional affront to guilty and innocent alike, and doubly so to those who must do business there five or six days a week.

"One cannot help it if the human mind has a tendency to associate truth with light, justice with audibility, efficiency with ample room, and if light woodwork and new paint stimulate positivism and dark woodwork and old paint do not.

"It is easy to believe that the rays of the sun, on the best day in July, cannot — perhaps would not even dare — penetrate this gloomy structure that persists in living beyond its time."

And of course, there are the annual holidays, special occasions and seasons. This is spring:

"At the upper end of the orchard, the 60-year-old apple tree leaned like an overburdened ship in a gale. The winters, not excluding the last one, which had piled drifts branch-high against its twisted trunk had so warped, knotted and gnarled its 'treeness' as to make it appear more caricature than real.

"Yet in the bright sun, a robin, somewhat pale of breast but eager to get on with the business of spring, sang from a weathered branch. And coming close, there already were signs that the branch itself, with a fine mixture of poetry and industry, was preparing to burst into flower when it got ready.

"This is the season of which the Venerable Bede wrote in the eighth century: 'It is the time when the old festival is observed with the gladness of a new solemnity.' "

Go well and write well, remembering that there are few subjects indeed that cannot be represented in readable fashion if you are willing to think before you write. And *do* write an occasional anemone — it's good for you.

This article, published in the March 1982 Bulletin, is adapted from remarks Allen delivered to the 1981 convention of the National Conference of Editorial Writers.

Overcoming obstacles to better newswriting

Roy Peter Clark

Gene Patterson plucked me out of a snug English department office last June and plunked me into the middle of the St. Petersburg Times newsroom. He then described what was to become my year's labors in the newspaper business: "I want you to learn all about this business. I want you to improve the quality of the writing here at the Times. And I want you to find ways by which *any* newspaper can improve its writing." Then, his jaw set with determination, he went on vacation.

Thus abandoned in the newsroom, I had no choice but to meet reporters and editors on their own terms. I accompanied reporters to dull courtroom trials and duller county commission meetings. I watched them write three stories in an hour. I sat in the press box during a Tampa Bay Buccaneer loss (until early December a tautology), and I marvelled as our sportswriters banged out lines of able prose under an oppressive deadline. I worked for a month on the copydesk, absorbing the experience of editors as they gave muscles to flabby prose.

I learned a few valuable lessons right away: that newspaper writing is better than most academic writing, that a newspaper contains individuals of widely varying abilities, that few agree on what constitutes "good" newspaper writing, that newspaper writers have fragile egos and that reporters and editors love to blame each other for the weaknesses in newspaper writing.

In my first weeks at the paper, I heard a story about a midwestern editor who had developed his own way of improving the writing at his paper. He would throw his telephone at a writer who made a grammatical error. The mistake was rarely repeated.

Although I've had the urge to throw a phone — sometimes a telephone pole — at a college student who refused to make subject and verb agree, I know that is *not* the way to encourage good writing. I do not believe in holding a writer's work up to ridicule or in burdening a student's paper with dozens of redpencilled corrections that are inevitably ignored.

For complicated reasons, many college students can barely write. At times I will wait for weeks until I find the sentence I am looking for in the work of a student. "Yes. It has a subject and a verb. Subject and verb agree! The sentence is clear. And interesting. That's it: one, good standard English sentence. If you can do it once, you can do it again and again."

I brought this philosophy of teaching to the newsroom: Get the writer to recognize and emulate his own strengths. Unlike college students, reporters write every day. They write with a purpose. And they write for an audience of editors and readers. They have a professional stake in improving their skills. For these reasons, I find the newsroom more fertile than the classroom for cultivating a writer's skills.

Before I tacked my newspaper writing theses on Gene Patterson's door, I wanted to interview every writer on the staff, a process that lasted four months. I preferred one-on-one sessions to group meetings. These were, after all, professionals, and I wanted to avoid a "classroom" setting that might make some writers uncomfortable. I would use these interviews to get to know the strengths and weaknesses of each writer, to make each one think more about writing as a craft, and to suggest one or two specific remedies to improve the writer's style.

To prepare for the interviews, I reviewed about six months of articles from byline files and sought out editors' opinions on a writer's work. I looked carefully to find examples of strong writing : a good lead, an effective transition, even a single interesting word.

At a typical interview I might ask some of the following questions:

Where did you learn to write? How long have you covered your beat? How do your editors react to your work? Do they rewrite your stories? How do you feel about that? After a story appears in print, do the editors ever criticize your work? Has anyone at the paper ever praised your writing? What have you been reading lately? Which writers do you admire? What are your writing habits? How do you handle deadline pressure? Do you rewrite much? If you do rewrite, what changes will you make?

Then the questions become more specific.

Do you think about the length of your sentences? How do you use direct quotations? Do you have problems incorporating attribution smoothly into a story? Do you find yourself using cliches as a result of covering (government, sports, police) for so long? What do you try to accomplish in a lead? What was the best lead you ever wrote? Do you pay attention to the types of verbs that you use? Do you ever think of the overall structure of your article? About transitions? Do you rely on the inverted pyramid? Do you spend as much time with endings as you do leads?

The reporter does most of the talking. After a free-wheeling bull-session that might last as long as two hours, we will browse through the byline file. I let the writer pick up a story at random and comment on problems he might have faced in writing it. I find an opportunity to point out specific strengths: "That lead works because you used two sentences instead of one" or "You have a way of dropping key facts into the story without obstructing the flow" or "That passage is concise because you use active verbs."

About half the writers I interviewed could not describe the distinction between active and passive verbs, even though most of them wrote with active verbs all the time. I would use the opportunity for some informal instruction.

In the days after the interview I would discuss a writer's work with him whenever I got the chance, perching on the edge of his desk to exchange some ideas on a recent article. I am happy to say that after the interview many writers would seek me out to discuss problems with a story, to bitch about an editor or headline writer or to argue a point of usage. I also tried to work on an article with the writer, to concentrate on the *process* of writing as well as on the *product*.

The ability of the writers varied so greatly that no single interview proceeded in a set pattern. Some I talked with were accomplished newspaper writers and novelists. Others wrote ungrammatical prose. My goal was to raise the awareness of each writer about the *craft* of writing. I never attempt to force a writer into radical stylistic changes. When appropriate, I might suggest one or two changes: "Don't always write one-sentence leads" or "Don't begin so many sentences with *it is* or *there are*" or "Don't feel you always have to cram the attribution into the lead."

Four months of meetings with writers and editors and visits to other newspapers have led to a series of preliminary conclusions which I presented to Gene Patterson in October:

A writing consultant cannot singlehandedly improve the quality of the writing at a newspaper. The push must come from the bigshots at a paper and the editors who handle copy every day. When a writer comes to a newspaper, he must learn quickly that he is entering an environment in which good writing is encouraged and rewarded. Long after the name of the writing consultant is a whisper in the wind, writers and editors will be working together to produce good writing for the Times.

Newspapers don't give enough emphasis to good writing. They think more about accuracy, fairness, privacy, libel, advertising, circulation and design. "We don't call them writers," said a New York editor, "we call them reporters. Oh, I was at a paper that had two writers once. They sat in a corner and talked to each other."

Writers don't rewrite enough. They have abdicated that responsibility to editors. At times the deadline makes rewriting impossible. But writers often use the deadline as a scapegoat. They get in the habit of writing quickly and will organize their time to avoid rewriting. Perhaps an editor will discourage a writer from rewriting because revisions slow the writer.

But I have found that the better writers at a newspaper revise their work, refine their style and struggle to find just the right word. Rick Abrams, one of our best feature writers, will rewrite a lead 20 or 30 times, working on the flow and rhythms of his prose. Reporter Joe Childs compiles a list of interesting words as he covers an event so that he can accurately and colorfully recreate the event for his readers. Outdoors writer Jeff Klinkenberg will return to his office after interviewing a hunter or fisherman and rewrite his quotations in the order he wishes to use them. These writers know the *insides* of the words they use. They are good reporters. They rewrite. And it shows.

Editors hurt prose as often as they help it. I have seen an editor save a writer from an embarrassing mistake. I have praised many leads that had been radically rewritten by deskmen. But too few editors have nurtured a love for the language. They are not attuned to the subtle rhythms of prose or to the full power of language. Mike O'Neill, editor of the New York News, once told his editors to "wear blindfolds" and start *listening* for good writing. To appreciate good writing an editor has to "grow ears."

Some editors feel an editorial imperative which forces them to rewrite any passage that flashes across their VDTs. This is like unto a committee of the Anglican Church that decided to rewrite the Lord's Prayer. "Thy will be done on earth as it is in heaven" became "Your will be done on earth as in heaven." This represents the kind of change many editors would make. William F. Buckley Jr. sees this as proof that "A venerable passage will be reworded by a rewording commission insofar as a commission to reword possesses the authority to do so."

Editors need not be great writers to do their work effectively. But they should be able to recognize good writing when they see it. There are times when the best response to a writer's work is a round of applause.

Editors do not spend enough time with their best writers. This may seem to contradict my previous point, but I don't think it does. Most editors expend a great deal of energy improving weak writing — just to get it in the paper. When they get a good article from a writer, they are so relieved that they do not give the article the attention it deserves. Editors often miss the opportunity to turn a good article into an excellent one and to refine a good writer's skills.

Editors do not offer writers enough helpful criticism. Too often changes are made without the knowledge of the writer. And when changes are made, the editor offers no explanation as to how the changes improve the story. This reflects a general abandoning of the teaching role by editors. I am told that the burden of writing instruction has traditionally fallen on editors. It was an editor of the young James J. Kilpatrick who sent him this valuable memo: ". . . Those interesting objects are known as periods. You do not seem to be well acquainted with them. I urge you to try a few. You will find the key that produces them on the bottom row of your typewriter, toward the right-hand end."

A modern editor recently said of his paper, "We are not an educational institution. We assume that people know how to write when they get here." By the looks of some of the writing in his paper, he is wrong.

Because newspapers are concerned with tomorrow's product, editors rarely review yesterday's writing. They fail to congratulate a writer for an effective story or to consider why a particular lead did not work or why a transition did not hold a piece together. Editors should occasionally peruse byline files. They can remind a writer how well he did last year and how much better he should be doing next year.

Writers and editors stereotype the reader. A lot of formula writing results from an unfortunate characterization of the abilities and interests of the "typical reader." We find out that he has the reading ability of an eighth-grader, or that he will not read any sentence longer than 12 words, or that he will never read more than five paragraphs into a story. When I hear these self-fulfilling prophecies, I am reminded of E.B.

White's statement that "writing is an act of faith, not a trick of grammar." I often dispense the advice of William Zinsser: "Write for yourself." The writer must have faith that good writing will not be lost on his reader, that some seed will fall on fertile as well as rocky ground.

I presented a plan to Gene Patterson which would build into the newspaper an atmosphere conducive to good writing. I wanted to get everyone concerned about good writing and interesting language. I considered this an effort in "Lone Ranger diplomacy": To create a situation in which I am no longer needed. In June of 1978 I want everyone to look off into the distance and ask, "Who was that masked man?"

To accomplish this I introduced the paper to some new items:

The Wind Bag: For the last two months I've published this weekly newsletter on writing. The prototype for this three-page memo is Ted Bernstein's "Winners & Sinners." But The Bag differs from Bernstein's sheet in both tone and emphasis. The Bag does contain specific, technical problems of usage, the nuts and bolts of last week's paper. But it also discusses broader stylistic problems. I use The Bag to encourage good writing and to publicly praise the writing and editing skills of the Times. The Bag also accepts submissions from all staffers. We debate questions of usage and style. There is art and humor in The Bag. After only eight editions, I find that people are writing to get in The Wind Bag — and also to stay out of it.

The Writers' Lunch: Newspaper writers often forget how good newspaper writing can be. To remedy this I pick out an excellent article that illustrates effective writing techniques. Some of these come from well known writers such as Breslin, Mailer, Updike or Willie Morris. Others are from lesser-known writers. We have averaged crowds of 25 persons, an interesting mixture of writers, editors and others. There is always a debate. When the opportunity arises I direct the discussion to our own paper: "Would the Times print this story?" or "Have you read any editorials in our paper which were as persuasive as this one?"

Deadline Questions: You can lead a writer to a copy of a Bernstein book or Strunk & White's *Elements of Style.* But you can't make him read it. The writer can benefit from the wisdom in these works, but I have found that a reporter under deadline rarely applies the advice of the experts to his daily work.

I do not believe you can reduce good writing to rules. As Mencken says, "A style is always the outward and visible symbol of a man, and it cannot be anything else. To attempt to teach it is as silly as to set up courses in making love." Strunk & White meet Masters & Johnson.

But I compiled this short list of questions to encourage writers to rewrite more and to remind everyone that good writing is not a freak of nature but depends upon careful rewriting. Since these are not "rules" of good writing, they will not guarantee any dramatic improvements. But if a reporter has never thought seriously about the elements of effective newspaper writing, this list will give him a start.

This then is a history of my first half year at the St. Petersburg Times. Tune in about six months from now to get my final report on Gene Patterson's daring project. But let me relieve some of the suspense. I see evidence that the interviews, memos, lunches and many daily informal meetings are working. Some mornings I read the paper and feel like Sisyphus after his stone has rolled down the hill. But I am rewarded on other days when I see signs of life from writers who have been hibernating for years in the Cave of Hacks.

Deadline Questions

Have I used verbs in the active voice? "It was announced by Patterson that the writing would be improved by Clark" becomes "Patterson announced that Clark would improve the writing."

Are subjects close to verbs? "Bothwell, after skulking about the newsroom and peeking over Eleazer's shoulder, stole ideas for his column" becomes "Skulking about the newsroom and peeking over Eleazer's shoulder, Bothwell stole ideas for his column."

Have I avoided long, unreadable sentences? Go back and break them in two for clarity and readability, for when sentences run too long and when they get too complicated you often find that the reader will find them hard to follow and just give up on the whole goddam thing rather than to struggle from the starting block of a capital letter to that period which looks like the dark at the end of the tunnel — when your sentences are too long, that is.

Does my article have a beginning, a middle and an end? Don't just stack the facts. Tell a story. Help the reader through the story with good transitions. Give the reader a sense of completion with a good ending.

Have I sought alternatives to cliches? Or does my copy read "In the wake of the death of an underworld figure who came under fire from the mob, a reputed Mafia kingpin was struck down in a bowling alley?"

Have I cluttered my lead with needless attribution, confusing statistics or bureaucratic names? "Thursday the South Largo Subcommittee on Historic Preservation and Reclamation received grants totaling $453,100 over a six-year period to help restore 23 houses which date back to the early 1800's, F. Ralph Gross, executive vice-president and deputy coordinator of administrative services, said Friday."

Have I cut out needless words, especially modifiers? "~~After a while, the sorrowful~~ Jesus ~~in a startling development~~ wept ~~quite a bit.~~"

ROY PETER CLARK, director of the Modern Media Institute's writing seminars, contributed this article to the February 1978 Bulletin.

Column writing

On being oneself, not Jimmy Breslin

Richard Cohen

It is an historic, but not necessarily a gripping fact that about four years ago the National Park Service considered replacing the mules that pull the barges on Washington's C & O Canal with diesel engines and that this more or less coincided with my debut as a columnist. I was not particularly fond of the mules, but the decision to replace them with some smelly machine did not strike me as right and moreover — and much more to the point — I needed a column. Not for the first time, the mules were conscripted for a cause.

I went down to the C & O Canal, even though I had been there many times before and, in fact, used to live nearby. I did this because I was new at column-writing and still believed in the value of intensive reporting qua reporting, although, to tell the truth, I was not sure I needed any of it. All I wanted to say was that replacing mules with diesel engines was a lousy idea.

Anyway, I walked along the canal. It was a nice day in the early spring, and the barge rides had not yet begun for the season. There were no tour guides to interview, no mule skinners, no mules and, really, no people. I walked and walked and then went back to the office and called everyone in the National Park Service. In fact, I reported the hell out of the story, wrote the column and was about to turn it in when someone from the National Park Service called. The decision had been reversed. The mules would stay.

It was a lesson. The fact is that much of life is like that column about the mules. Life simply will not conform to 20 inches and punchy endings. Sometimes there is no point. A column has to have a point and in the case of the mules, I had simply lost it. (You cannot rail against something that hasn't happened.) Some things just are. They are funny or tragic or whatever, but try as you might you cannot make sense of them.

But it is the duty of the columnist to do just that. It is the duty of the local columnist to take news, which is to say life, and make a point with it. In the copy, people have to talk colorfully. You have to take news and turn it into entertainment, give it a beginning, a middle and an end. Just like television.

You cannot end a cops-and-robbers show on television by saying that no one could figure out who committed the murder and no one cared anyway. You can't do this with a column, either.

And so when I was writing this sort of column, the sort of local column, I would do my reporting and then my writing and then, over and over again, the writing. I would hone and sandpaper until I got the thing into some sort of shape where I could say something — make a point. If I couldn't do that, I knew I had failed that day. I knew it and, I sensed, the readers knew it. They weren't reading me for news. They wanted a lesson, a point — entertainment.

There are two persons who can do this consistently and well — albeit quite differently. They are Mike Royko and Jimmy Breslin and, between the two of them, they have been the ruin of more young columnists than booze or drugs or fat contracts from television. Royko and Breslin are what all editors want, but God didn't make but two of them. They are what they are and that is, in their own way, very gifted. With both you get more than just a point or a statement. At the very least, you get a wonderful eye — a way of seeing things. They are magnificently talented men and they cannot be duplicated.

But God how people try. Editors know what they want. They want what they have read elsewhere. They want someone to go out every day and report a story and come back with a column. They want life to conform to the dictates of column-writing and they don't want to be told that it cannot be done. They want Breslin. They want Royko. Trouble is, they're already working elsewhere.

I consider myself lucky. No one ever told me who to be, but I thought I knew what was expected. And so I tried. I tried to be Breslin. I tried real hard. I read Breslin and whenever I did, I wound up writing like him. Instead of writing Washington, I wrote "the City of Washington." (Like Hemingway, he is easy to imitate, impossible to duplicate.) I read Royko and the same thing happened. I'd sit down at the typewriter and ersatz Royko would come out. I met a cop and I thrilled at the opportunity to turn him into my own working-class folk figure. Like Breslin did. Like Royko did. He would be my Slats Grobnick. He would be my Marvin the Torch. Trouble was, he never said anything colorful. All he talked about was his pension.

People suggested I make things up. They said Breslin must do that. They said Royko must do that. They said create someone like Fat Thomas. I said, whatja mean create? I met Fat Thomas! Jimmy Breslin brought him to the Columbia Graduate School of Journalism when I was a student there. (Despite this, some people still think Columbia is a classy place.)

I stopped reading Breslin. I stopped reading Royko. I read Pete Hamill — I thought he read like Breslin and so I had to stop reading Hamill, too. Everywhere I turned, there were clones of Breslin and Royko and I imagined city editors standing over young men just out of Ivy League colleges saying, "Jesus kid, don't you know someone colorful?" Well, the fact was that I didn't. And it gradually occurred to me that if I was going to stay in the column biz, writing three a week, I had to be me. I could not be Breslin or Royko, but more than that, or aside from that, my city, like most cities, was not New York or Chicago. Washington just is not a blue-collar town. In Washington, Fat Thomas would have slimmed down at the Y.

In fact, I concluded that the Washington area (or many other cities) was a lot like me. It was middle-class and it ate in restaurants and it read books and worried about the schools and whether the sexually liberated man was Alan Alda or Hugh Hefner. (It's Alda. Okay, it's Hefner.) It was not a city where men stopped off at bars for a pop on the way home from work, and it was too fragmented, too new, too much composed of new immigrants, for a columnist to make an all-but-mythical character out of the Mayor of the District of Columbia. (His name is Marion Barry and when he was elected, a network newscaster stationed here called him "her.")

So, in the sense that Royko personifies a certain side of Chicago and Breslin is New York (which is to say Queens County) to the quick, I set out to be something I had never been in print — me. I was going to be me on the hunch that I was more like Washington than, say, Breslin was, and also because if you're going to write three times a week, it is easier to do it as yourself than as someone else. I wrote, therefore, about taking my kid for a haircut in a town where all the barbershops have been replaced by unisex hair parlours — not even parlors. I wrote about hiring a clown for a birthday party and not knowing whether to tip him. I wrote about sex a lot, because it bothers us all a lot and because I think about it a lot and because it is one way social change becomes evident. I wrote about gay people and battered wives and men and women who felt alienated from both each other and themselves.

I wrote about television violence and television sex and just plain television. I wrote about the movies and books and cars and vacations. I wrote about getting a date for New Year's Eve and why Labor Day is really New Year's and how teenagers could manage to stay chaste. (Get acne.) I wrote about politics, sure, and international events and the things I felt important. I went to the Middle East and to Poland and to the national political conventions, not to get the story behind the story, but because some things need to be seen to be understood. I also wrote about poverty, civil liberties, welfare, discrimination, racism, human rights, the death penalty — issues that mattered a lot to me.

But basically the conventional reporting I did was limited. I worked hard at talking to others and especially at thinking — at asking myself over and over again the same question: What does this mean? Sometimes, the meaning of an event, of a news story, of a social development, was instantly clear and I would know right off what I wanted to say. Sometimes, though, I would only know that the subject interested me, that I wanted to learn more about it, say something about it, and the meaning of it all might only become clear in the writing. I have a writer's prejudice about writing. To me, it is a form of thinking.

Most of the time I think I do all right at this sort of column. Sometimes I fail. But the reader, by and large, has stayed with me. I have not written down to him or her and I have not tried to be clever with them and most of all have tried to be me and no one else. It happened not a moment too soon. The Park Service mules still make me shudder.

It was only a matter of time until I interviewed them.

RICHARD COHEN writes a thrice-weekly column for The Washington Post that is nationally syndicated. This article was first published in the November 1981 Bulletin.

Ten Commandments of press columny

William Safire

Looking for a formula to start a hot new newspaper column? Here are Ten Commandments of Columny, any deviation from which spells certain doom.

1. Skip the first six months. During this period, readers always say, "You call this a column? This is a mishmash." That is because they are unfamiliar with the neophyte pundit's style, if he has any style. Later, when readers get used to the new columnist, they say, "He's learning. He's hitting his stride. I like him now." Much later, they will tell him, "I like you now, but boy, was your stuff terrible at first." The only solution is to skip the first six months.

2. Avoid even-numbered thinking. One idea is a column. Trying to fit two ideas into one column tells the reader you couldn't decide what to write about that day. However, three ideas is a pattern, a gestalt, a farrago that illuminates the point, as long as the ideas are related. Four ideas and the column falls apart again. Nobody knows why even numbers are the columnist's curse, but it is probably why "The Four Modernizations" failed in China.

3. Write 110 percent of what you know. In the Lippmann era, pundits wrote less than half of what they knew; in the recent past, thumbsuckers were forced to write all they knew lest the reporters caught up with them; today, the compleat columnist cannot limit himself to what he knows. The secret is to go to the limits of knowledge, and then say you are guessing; sophisticated readers will assume you are not guessing, but are only claiming to guess to cover a source. There is no coverup like the truth.

4. Stick a profundity at the end of a paragraph near the middle of the column. This will trip skimmers; no political column worth its salt may be skimmed. The profundity need not be related to the central idea of the column as long as it is brief, declarative and opaque. Example: "There is no coverup like the truth."

5. Create your own "constituency of the infuriated" at the outset. Readers no longer turn to columnists to tell them what to think; rather, they turn to writers who cause them to say, "Why do they print this drivel? How can anybody think like this?" The only regular reader today is the irritated reader, and the most successful column is one that causes the reader to throw down the paper in a peak of fit.

6. *Put the story in the tail.* Seek out some delicious tidbit of news with which to make your column talked about. Then scorn journalism-school adjurations and slip the news in half-way between the profundity and the snapper. The columnist who calls attention to his news, loses: The winner treats news offhandedly, as if everybody should know it. News-burying also embarrasses op-ed page editors who take the column and snip off the end to make it fit the page; in time, they learn to snip off the lead.

7. *Stand against something.* Insist that politicians stand "for" something, and when they do, stand foursquare against it. "Pro" writing is pleading, handwringing, goody-goody, the work of apologists. "Con" writing is sprightly, vituperative, quotable, the product of writers uncorrupted by originality. No punch has the punch of a counterpunch. (Avoid two profundities in one column, but three is okay.)

8. *Specialize in being a generalist.* The new columnist should not begin with two columns on a single subject lest he be slotted for life in that category. If you open with the significance of the population explosion in Ulan Bator, follow with a heartwarmer about nuclear reactors in Dayton and quickly shift to a rip-snorter about the gold standard. Versatility is all: Every new columnist must be able to thrill the new customers with his expert-tease.

9. *Carry a big schtick.* Every column must have its special characteristic: Evans and Novak's secret meetings, Reston's long view, Will's quotations, Kilpatrick's fulminations, McGrory's heavenward eye-rollings, Safire's italicized enumerations, Buckley's self-mocking rodomontade. A reader should be able to identify a column without its byline or funny little picture on top — purely by look or feel, or its turgidity ratio. (One device waiting to be used is the printing of untruths in boldface type permitting the reader to expostulate "That's a boldfaced lie!")

10. *Write tight.* A new columnist must go through the verbosity bends, coming to the surface with his original thought or illuminating insight squeezed into exactly 800 words. He must remind himself that the Gettysburg Address ran 266 words and

"fourscore and seven" could have been shrunk to "87." Nor can he run short, lest laidback layout men be forced to scramble for fillers. The trick is to bring it in on the button. Right on the 800-word button, not one word more or less. There.

WILLIAM SAFIRE's twice weekly political column in The New York Times earned him a Pulitzer Prize for distinguished commentary in 1978. This article was published in the November 1981 Bulletin.

Stitching together piffle and profundities

Herb Caen

There is nothing like reading an obituary about yourself while you are still, presumably, alive. Or at least, breathing in and out with reasonable regularity. This pleasantly mordant thought crossed my mind when that estimable New York fishwrap, The Village Voice, published an Alexander Cockburn piece about me titled, "A Dying Breed: The Last of the Three-Dot Columnists" ... Cockburn is pronounced "Co-burn." This has nothing to do with the preceding remarks. It's simply the way three-dot columnists operate. They are easily ... distracted. They also subscribe to the gossipel as enunciated by the grand-daddy of us all, Walter Winchell. "People don't get bored," Walter the Winch assured me, "if you change the subject often enough." I don't know if that's true or not. Before we get into a boring discussion of his remark, let's change the subject, okay?

Getting back to The Village Voice, I may be dying but I am not the last of the three-dot columnists. The winsome Liz Smith in New York and Irv Kupcinet and Aaron Gold in Chicago come readily to mind, and there are others all around the land, stitching together piffle and profundities with those three little dots, otherwise known as ellipses or even, in old printerese, "extenders."

Nevertheless, this is not the golden age of three-dot journalism. It sickens me to report that some highly successful papers — The New York Times, The Washington Post, The Boston Globe, Los Angeles Times and a pox on them all — get by without a single three-dotter, may their tribe decrease. To me, this makes them less fun to read, but I am not an impartial observer. Most of us colyummists (that's Winchellingo) write the kind of columns we like to read, and I think three dots are the way to go. They sort of pull your eyes along from one caenanity to the next ... and before you know it, you've read the whole column, and none the wiser for it, too.

There was a time, dear ones, when the newspaper business, especially in Manhattan, was chockablock with three-dot columnists. Maybe The Winch didn't invent the form, but he certainly popularized it, and did it better than anyone else, ever. His column had the flavor of Broadway, the beat of the big city. WW in his prime was full of pith and vinegar, his column loaded with one-liners and scoops, half of them true.

When Winchell came along, circa 1930, O.O. (for Oscar Odd) McIntyre was the king of the Broadway columnists, but our hero knocked him out of the box. McIntyre used short items, too, but NO DOTS. Therein lay the seeds of his own destruction. Winchell was off and rolling, followed by a long line of instant imitators: Ed Sullivan, Danton Walker, Louis Sobol, Earl Wilson. Sullivan, who later became much more celebrated as a TV variety show host, was such a slavish copycat that Winchell once said:

"That Sullivan! He oughta get down on his knees alongside his bed every night and thank God there was a Walter Winchell." (Dramatic pause.) "Couldn't he at least give me back my three ... little ... dots?"

I turned dotty at an early age. In the early 1930's, when I was already embarked on a gossipy career as the "Corridor Gossip" columnist for the Sacramento High School X-Ray, I may have been the only person west of the Rockies to subscribe to the New York Daily Mirror — just so I could read The Original Winchell (the late San Francisco Call-Bulletin ran him, too, but expurgated). I got so adept at mimicking his rat-a-tat-tat style that when I first met the great man himself, at the Stork Club, he turned to Owner Sherman Billingsley and said, "This kid imitates me better than anybody in the business."

Winchell meant it as a compliment, and I took it as such. It was only later, when his politics turned sourly to the right, that I fell out of love with The Bard of Broadway, a.k.a. The Gray Ghost of Gotham. Still, in his prime, he was a wonder.

When the late Editor Paul C. Smith — almost everybody I knew and admired is "late" — gave me my column in 1938, he issued only one caveat: "Keep it entertaining. Keep it short. And remember one thing — I am easily bored." Even now, long after Paul's death, when I embark on a longish essay, I can hear Paul yelling down from that great city room in the sky, "Ferkrissakes change the subject, you're boring hell out of me!"

I think the reason there are so few three-dot columnists today, especially young ones, is that the genre requires hard work. Instead of expanding airily on a theme, you have to boil a story down, preferably to one sentence in which every word counts. My favorite short item: "... Norman Jewison isn't. ..."

Of course, a lot of readers didn't understand that one, but who cares? That is the perfect three-dot item. A daily column of from 15 to 25 items is drudgery, but worth it. If the items are strong, and the writing taut, and the one-liners sharp, there is no more satisfying journalistic device.

Some years ago, when the Los Angeles Times lost two of its local columnists, the late Paul Coates and Matt Weinstock, the editors searched the country, the campuses and the college papers, trying to find someone who'd write the so-called "item" column. No takers. Too much work. "We talked to a lot of bright young writers," sighed Jim Bassett, "but they want to pontificate. They all want to be Reston or Buckley."

My greatest tribute as a three-dotter came from Phil Warner, the editor of the Houston Chronicle, which has been buying my column for years. When I finally met the chap, at a newspaper editors' convention, I asked, "My column is so LOCAL — why in the world do you buy it?" "Great filler stuff," he said. "With those three dots, you can cut the damn thing anywhere."

I can live with it. Cut my column anywhere or throw the damn thing away. Just BUY it . . . I thank you from the bottom of my dots . . .

HERB CAEN of the San Francisco Chronicle has been writing six columns a week for over two decades. This article was published in the November 1981 Bulletin.

Writers' tools

The bastardization
of our mother tongue

Wallace Carroll

The myths and illusions of the Age of Innocence are going fast. We Americans have now found out that bigger is not really better: Life in our cities would be so much better if we had kept the cities from growing so big. We have discovered too that education is not wisdom: Too many of our professors and students have learned to argue before they have learned to reason. Even our image of the American soldier as a kind of universal ambassador, a friend of children and a welcome visitor beloved by all has now been shattered by the events in Vietnam.

One of our cherished myths, however, has endured. It is Emerson's law. There may be some dispute about the words, but the popular version is authentic enough: "If a man can write a better book, preach a better sermon or make a better mousetrap than his neighbor, though he builds his house in the woods, the world will make a beaten path to his door."

Emerson undoubtedly was right in his day, but does his wisdom still hold true? I doubt it. In fact, something like Emerson's law in reverse now seems to prevail in our country:

• If a company can build a flashier car that will burn more premium gasoline to go a shorter distance than most others, Americans young and old will beat a four-lane path to the showroom door.

• If some enemy of the human race can concoct something even less toothsome than the roadside hamburger, businessmen will bid for a franchise, neon-lighted shacks will tout the stuff from ocean to ocean and the stock of the reprobate's company will go up, up, up on the New York Stock Exchange.

• If an artist of sorts can paint something even less fascinating than a can of tomato soup, the Guggenheim will give him an exhibit, Life magazine will hail him as a folk genius and millionaires will hang his pictures on their apartment walls from Park Avenue to Nob Hill.

• And if a playwright can turn out a play about a romance between a scrofulous lady acrobat and a homosexual chimpanzee, Broadway will put his name on the marquee, Hollywood will pay millions for the film rights and Jack Valenti, the arbiter of everything true and beautiful on the screen, will give the picture a "G" rating and release it for the Christmas season so that all the family together may enjoy its wholesome message.

Let us pursue this depressing realization to a point nearer home — to the realm of words and images.

Here, too, Emerson is in full retreat. All of us know that if an obscure man can take two clear, simple words like "hot" and "cool" (words that cannot be misunderstood even by a retarded four-year old), and if that man can so twist and mangle those words that everybody in his right mind will wonder what in the name of McLuhan he means by them — if a man can do this he will be hailed as a genius in "communications"; foundations will shower grants upon him and a university chair will be richly endowed for him so he can perpetuate his befuddlement among succeeding generations.

The farther we go on from this point and explore what is happening to spoken and written English, the more we see that Emerson has become obsolete. Emerson's law has indeed become *Nosreme's* law. And if you wonder who this Nosreme is, he is, of course, only poor old Emerson in reverse. Thus we can confidently state Nosreme's law as it applies today to the use of the English language: If a man can write muddier prose than his neighbor, if he can arrange words in ways that befuddle the brain and grate on the ear, he will never have to monkey with a better mousetrap.

Do you want to be recognized as an authority on reading in the public schools? Then you have only to write like this:

"Perhaps the task of developing proper motivation is best seen, at least in a nutshell, as limiting the manipulation of extrinsic factors to that of keeping homeostatic need and exteroceptic drive low, in favor of facilitating basic information processing to maximize accurate anticipation of reality."

Do you want to become a professor of the behavioral sciences in a great university? Then you simply need to express yourself in this way:

"If the correlation of intrinsic competency to actual numerical representation is definitely high, then the thoroughly objective conclusion may inexpugnably be reached that the scholastic derivations and outgrowths will attain a pattern of unified superiority."

Do you want to become the chief of a government bureau? Then learn to write and talk like this:

"The Board's new regulatory goal is to create a supervisory

*environment conducive and stimulative to industry adaptation
to its fundamentally altered markets. We will give you the op-
tions to restructure both sides of your statement of condition, but
the decision-making and the long-range planning function is
management's....We will look to you for input of information
which we shall rely on in making our decisions."*

This bastardization of our mother tongue is really a disaster
for all of us in the news business. The English language is our
bread and butter, but when ground glass is mixed with the
flour and grit with the butter, our customers are likely to lose
their appetite for what we serve them.

Our job is to interpret — to translate. Yet our translators
— that is our reporters and copy editors — find it more and
more difficult to do this basic job of translation. To begin with,
they reach us from universities that are tending to become glo-
rified jargon factories; and for four years or more they have
been immured in a little cosmos where jargon is too often
mistaken for knowledge or wisdom. Besides, no matter what
their beat may be, their ears are battered every day with the
specialized jargon that each branch of human activity now uses
to glorify or disguise its handiwork.

Thus, if we take the reporter on the school beat, we find that
he is likely to be writing about underachievers, environmental
deprivation, innovative teaching techniques and restructured
curricula. And if we skip from him all the way to the man on
the White House beat, we find him wallowing in escalation and
de-escalation (just use the prefix "de" to get the antonym of any
word), nuclear proliferation, viable alternatives, dichotomous
jurisdictions and meaningful dialogues.

Before I belabor outsiders any further for what they are doing to the language, I want to deal with some of the barriers to
good newswriting that we erect against ourselves. Some of
these barriers take the form of unwritten laws handed down by
anonymous oracles long before William Randolph Hearst was
running around San Francisco in short pants.

There are all kinds of taboos involving words or ways of writing on every newspaper. Today no one knows how they started
and no one asks whether they still have validity. And then
there are all the awkward ways of saying things that origi-
nated in the Dark Ages and that we keep on using without ever
asking why. Take the "breech-delivery lead" — the story that
comes at the reader rear end foremost:

Washington (AP)— Although one-third of some 600 citizens

hadn't heard about Vice President Spiro T. Agnew's much-publicized dispute with the television networks, he's "a household name" now, the Republican National Committee reported Friday.

". . . the Republican National Committee reported Friday." there are at least a half-dozen other ways to write that lead, and all of them better than this. But way back in the previous century, someone got the idea that the lead had more punch if you reversed the natural order of a sentence and put the source at the end. And, of course, the journalism schools concluded that this must be the way to write a news story because all the newspapers were doing it. So we have been doing it that way ever since.

Another way to make writing "punchy," according to our newsroom folklore, is to eliminate the "the's" and "a's" at the beginning of a sentence. So when the reader picks up his paper, he finds paragraphs starting like this:

Biggest manpower reduction comes in the Pacific command, where . . .

Did you ever hear anyone talk like that: "Biggest manpower reduction comes. . . ."? Of course not. No one has talked like that since Julius Caesar, and he, poor fellow, only talked that way because his Latin language did not have the definite and indefinite articles. But it is these little words that give English some of its grace and lilt, and we throw them away only at the risk of erecting an unnecessary barrier between ourselves and the reader, who is accustomed to them.

There is another construction more Latin than English that has also been favored since ancient times by lazy writers and lazy deskmen. That is, putting a participle or verb at the beginning of a sentence, thus: "Killed in the three-car collision was Hyman J. O'Connor . . . ." That way of writing or talking also went out with the Caesars. Can you imagine calling your wife some day and saying: "Brace yourself, dear. Dead on arrival at Baptist Hospital was your Aunt Agatha, 57"?

But that's the way we talk to our readers. Are we kidding them, or are we kidding ourselves?

Another fad — a more recent one — that is making much of our newswriting hard to savor is the elimination of prepositions. No one ever writes any more, "The Governor of New York" or "The Senator from Massachusetts." No, it is always "New York Gov." or "Massachusetts Sen." And this same fad, a product of sheer laziness, also brings us the piling up of identification in front of a name and the creation of bogus titles: "Belgian-born United States Army turncoat Albert Belhomme," or "Philadelphia Symphony tuba player Adrian Klotz."

All of these ancient shibboleths and latter-day fads conspire, then, to make the writing in our papers about as juicy as a Beltsville turkey (another proof, by the way, of Nosreme's law).

Now, what practical lessons can we draw?

First, we must resolve to check the alarming depreciation of our currency, the English language. We must nurture the talent we already have in our newsrooms and bring in more of those talented young people who have managed to go through college without acquiring a tin ear. And when we have brought them in we must not drill the talent out of them as we have done with so many before them: Tone-deaf editors and deskmen have always been the curse of our business.

Out the window must go the shibboleths, the taboos on fresh and apt words, the awkward ways of writing leads and paragraphs. We must encourage our people to observe with a fresh eye, listen with a receptive ear and write with a sensitive touch. I do not go along with those who now say, "Objectivity is out"; I do believe that *sensitivity* is "in" and sensitivity must come into play all along the line — in observing, in writing and in editing.

Secondly, we must instill into all our reporters, deskmen and editors a holy hatred of jargon. At every passgate there must be a watchman to keep it out of our columns. And while we stand on guard against the barbarisms of others, we must be still more vigilant against our own. You know many of these barbarisms — they are the pets of the lazy writer and lazy deskman. I shall list only a few. The lazy writer always:

puts "today" or the day of the week in front of the verb; piles up identification in front of the noun — ("Former North Carolina State basketball star, Larry Dugan," "Old-time square-dance master, Sam Queen");

says "burgeoning" when he means "growing" or "diminutive" when he means "little";

indulges in "elegant variation" — the vice that makes a house a "structure" and gold "the yellow metal";

uses "hike" when he means "rise" or "increase";

uses "warn" as an intransitive verb (Why do news sources never say anything; why do they always "warn"?);

strains to work in fad words — "relevant," "confrontation," "meaningful" and the haphazard "hopefully";

says future events are "upcoming";

delights in coining new expressions — "a piece of the action," "telling it like it is," "up tight."

You can add many more. For all such hideous and over-worked bromides and barbarisms, we should have only hatred and contempt.

Thirdly, we must — all of us — require better performance from our news services. The bad currency drives out the good, and the bad currency is slipping into our newsrooms every day over the press association wires. You may try as you will to improve your own standards, but unless we can do something about press association copy, you will be left standing there like little Peter with his finger in the dike with the chill waters rising all around you.

Now, I myself have been a press association hand and I know the pressures and handicaps under which the services operate. But I also know that I would have turned out better copy if one or two gentle editors had occasionally given me a well-directed kick in the pants. So I urge you to go over your wire copy with a gimlet eye and make your sentiments known.

For a start, you might look at your sports wires, taking as your inspiration this comment from the editorial page of The Wall Street Journal: "Why does anything that interests so many inspire such lousy writing?"

In Winston-Salem we take the AP sports wire, so I will make this bet: that if you will scan the weekend reports on the AP sports wire, you will agree with me there cannot possibly be any more cluttered, awkward, hard-to-read writing on the face of the earth, not even in Pravda and Izvestia.

What all this comes to in the end is pride — pride in our crafts-manship and pride in our craft. If we will take this kind of pride in our newswriting, the prose in our newspapers will be clean and lean and limber — which is the way it should be. And then there will be joy in the land, and people will actually read news-papers for pleasure. And in the fullness of time, Nosreme's law will in its turn be reversed, and somewhere out yonder, old Ralph Waldo Emerson will be heard to say: "Those ink-stained idiots — they really are making a better mousetrap."

WALLACE CARROLL, now retired, was editor and publisher of the Winston-Salem Journal and Sentinel. This article, an adaption of a speech to the New England Society of Newspaper Editors, appeared in the May 1970 Bulletin.

The problem of delinguancy

Theodore Bernstein

If there were such a word as delinguancy (and there certainly will be for the duration of this report at least), it might be defined as misbehavior with language. The misbehavior is not confined to juveniles nor to newspapermen. It is rife among all classes of language users. But, since newspapers use far more language than any other communication medium and since they exhibit it in permanent form (if breakfast table to garbage pail can be considered permanent), delinguancy in the press gives the appearance of being more prevalent than elsewhere and actually is more conspicuous.

This self-appointed cop has been on the delinguancy patrol for some years and is in a position to list the most common manifestations of misbehavior. If some of them seem piddling, it is probably because no connection is immediately apparent between the errors and really good writing. But the connection is there. It is not to be supposed that eliminating delinguant acts will automatically make a newspaperman a good writer, any more than eliminating delinquent acts will automatically make a street hooligan President. But on the other hand, no newspaperman who is habitually guilty of delinguancy can become a really good writer, just as no kid who persists in delinquency can become President.

Some of the terminology of delinquency can apply also to delinguancy. But whereas in the field of delinquency the terms state causes of misbehavior, in the field of delinguancy they name the offenses themselves. Here, then, is a handful of the most common delinguant acts that drive copy editors to the bourbon bottle:

Negligence, which often produces disagreement in number between subject and verb. Examples:

> The Navy announced that a task force, including an aircraft carrier, a cruiser and transports loaded with marines, *were* steaming southward.

> Under a new law limited licenses may be issued in cases where suspension of regular permits *work* occupational hardships on penalized drivers.

But the power, insight and heart of Mr. Cozzens' *By Love Possessed seems* to have eluded the scenarist. . .

These errors are ascribed to negligence rather than ignorance because it is assumed that even the lowliest of newspapermen have attended elementary school and can do simple sums. Oddly enough, these errors, which involve no esoteric grammatical principles, are the most prevalent of all.

Lack of balance, which causes misplacements when correlative conjunctions *(not only. . .but, neither. . .nor, both. . .and, etc.)* are employed. In the following examples the virgule (/) indicates where the *not only* and the *neither* should have been placed:

A broad program is under way not only to impress/Mr. Khrushchev but the Western peoples that the Western governments are serious.

Mr. Shapiro said he could not only produce/witnesses who saw the rat during the Mayor's visit, but also any number of students and teachers who had seen many other rats.

Mr. Newhouse, it is reported, neither attempts/to influence editorial opinions of his holdings nor to change their institutional character.

The principle underlying the proper placement of these words is one of logic: Correlative conjunctions must link parallel things. If the first element is followed by an infinitive, so must the second be; if the first element is followed by a noun, so must the second be, and so forth. It is really quite simple. Yet when you come across a *not only. . . but* in newspaper copy — or anywhere else, for that matter — you can bet your bottom buck that four times out of five there will be a misplacement.

Maladjustment, which attaches an unidiomatic preposition to a verb, noun or adjective. Examples:

A new ordinance goes into effect tomorrow forbidding residents of Rye *from* hanging laundry in their front yards.

Martin was accused in magistrate's court *with* assaulting a patrolman.

An aid to memory can be supplied here for *forbid*: Think of it as a matter of numbers — 4bid 2. But for the rest there are no rules, no principles. As is true of all idioms, they simply have to be known. An excellent list of prepositions, though, to be sure, it is not complete, appears in what must certainly be one of the most under-appreciated books ever published — *Words Into*

Type (Appleton-Century-Crofts).

Ignorance of the meanings of words, which leads to the use of *bastion* to mean merely a strong point, *comprise* to mean compose, *cohort* to mean an individual, *deprecate* to mean depreciate, *disinterested* to mean uninterested, *enormity* to mean enormousness, *flaunt* to mean flout, *fulsome* to mean full, *infer* to mean imply, *intrigue* to mean interest, *literally* to mean figuratively, *masterful* to mean masterly, *predicated* to mean based, *protagonist* to mean antagonist, *shambles* to mean a scene of wreckage, *transpire* to mean happen and *truculent* to mean aggressively defiant.

The list is, of course, by no means complete. And in addition to words that are used erroneously, there are many that are used loosely — for example, *jurist* for judge, *presently* for now, *publicist* for press agent, *realtor* for real estate dealer.

Overcrowding, particularly in lead paragraphs, which causes the reader to scratch his head in puzzlement or go back for a second reading or buy another newspaper. Examples:

Titan owner Harry Wismer yesterday cheerfully announced New York's AFL entry definitely will sign a new No. 2 quarterback before Sunday's Polo Grounds engagement with the Boston Patriots then, switching tunes without warning, he started blasting George Preston Marshall, owner of the NFL Redskins and his former football partner.

Ann McKiernan, the attractive brunette arrested as a cop-fighter after a brawl assertedly involving the teenage son of a South American official, will seek to subpoena 19-year-old Dario Avila despite his hand-me-down cloak of diplomatic immunity, her counsel disclosed yesterday.

In newspaper writing, where the goal must be above all to speed the reader on his way, there is no substitute for the simple sentence. And one way to achieve this is to confine each sentence to a single idea. No counting of words, no formulas are necessary. Just confine each sentence to a single idea, and length and simplicity will take care of themselves.

Quest for excitement, which leads to hot-rodding. In the tabloids especially, the simplest statements are jazzed up with adjectives, coined verbs, slang and ad hoc titles prefixed to names. Example:

Ex-con Heard Harden, burly 36-year-old former heavyweight pug who was convicted with disbarred attorney Burton Pugach in the lye-maiming of Pugach's exfiancee, Linda Riss, was haymakered with a 50-to-60-year sentence in Bronx County Court yesterday.

There is, of course, a violation of the tabloid rule book in that lead: No adjective describes Linda Riss. The book says that a woman must always be beautiful, shapely, attractive, comely, handsome, winsome, pretty or a charmer.

One of the most prevalent of the hot-rodding devices is the omission of an article at the beginning of a sentence: "Basis for most of the early projections of tightening credit was the expectation of a substantial upsurge in government spending. . . ." Suppose the sentence were to be turned around. Would the writer make it, "The expectation of a substantial upsurge in government spending was basis for, etc.?" Pretty obviously not. Let newswriters always remember the words of the Bible: "If I forget 'the,' O Jerusalem, let my right hand forget her cunning."

Obviously this rapid survey by no means exhausts the list of delinquancy offenses. Every editor will have his own *bête noire* to add to the menagerie here displayed. If the catalogue of faults has seemed to grow year by year, that fact can be largely ascribed, as can the growth of delinquency, to an underlying cause:

Disrespect for law. How, one may inquire, can there be respect for law if a large segment of the police force — i.e., teachers of English — is at pains to deny that there is any law? If a major premise of instruction asserts that correctness is a relative matter depending on levels of usage, what is there to teach and who needs teachers? Of course, to insist that grammar and usage are inflexible, unchanging and incapable of growth would be a ridiculous extreme, but no more ridiculous than the currently fashionable extreme of almost seeming to affirm that there are no rules of grammar and no code of usage and that the unlettered masses speak real good. At that extreme lies far more peril to the language than at the extreme of the conservative fuddy-duddies. And at that permissive extreme lie also the roots of today's delinquancy.

THEODORE BERNSTEIN, assistant managing editor of The New York Times, wrote this article for the November 1961 issue of The Bulletin. He died in 1979.

The blurring of
fact and fiction

David Shaw

Several years ago, I decided to write a story on the poker parlors of Gardena, the only community in the Los Angeles area in which gambling is legal. I've never been much of a gambler, but my dad and an aunt and uncle had spent day after day after day in Gardena during one prolonged period in my adolescence, and I'd been curious about the strange lure the poker tables held for them. So I proposed the idea to the editor, drew a $350 cash advance and began playing poker, day and night, in Gardena.

A couple of weeks later, I was talking to another reporter about my Gardena experiences, and he suggested that I write "a Cincinnati Kid kind of piece" for the paper.

"You know," he said, "take all those different people you met, all those colorful nicknames you mentioned — 'Ma' and 'Stumpy' and 'Loose Frank' and 'Dirty-Mouth Paula' — and write a story about one big showdown poker game, with you and all of them at one table. You could even combine a couple of the people into one, so it wouldn't be too unwieldy. You could use some of the anecdotes you saw and heard about and weave them into the game and build toward a big pot and — "

I interrupted him.

"Wait a minute. What you're suggesting is a splendid idea for a short story or a novel or a movie. But it's not journalism. You want me to *invent* a poker game that never happened, put characters in a situation they weren't in, with people they never met and create whole new, composite characters? Like you said, it's 'The Cincinnati Kid' — not a newspaper story."

My colleague looked as if I were daft. He looked, in fact, just as he had looked a month or so earlier, when he had been touting the celestial pleasures of LSD and I had shaken my head and muttered that I preferred a margarita. I was, in his enlightened view, hopelessly straight — a hidebound traditionalist in a time of soul-liberating experimentation.

I was indeed. In many ways, I still am.

I thought of this incident recently during all the furor over Janet Cooke's fabricated Washington Post story on a nonexistent, 8-year-old heroin addict. I have never met Janet Cooke, so can't presume to know what motivated her. I don't know if she, like my helpful colleague of a few years back, regarded journalism as just another literary form, something to be manipulated at will to produce a "higher truth." But I do worry that more reporters think this way today than most responsible journalists would like to admit. These "creative" reporters are still — thank Gutenburg — a tiny minority. But in today's media environment . . .

Docudramas. Faction. Nonfiction novels. Composites. Gonzo journalism. New journalism. The blurring of fact and fiction — of truth and invention — has become increasingly prevalent (and increasingly lucrative) in the past 15 or 20 years, and that worries me. A lot.

Yes, I know, writers have always taken truth — history — and rewritten it for dramatic purposes. Historians tell us that the real Richard III was certainly not the malevolent monster depicted by Shakespeare. Nor were the characters whom Hemingway described in *The Sun Also Rises* — recognizable though many of them were — faithful reproductions of real people. They were composites. Creations. Fact *and* fiction. But Hemingway wrote *novels*. Shakespeare wrote *plays*. Creative artists always draw on experience *and* imagination when they write. The reader knows that. But Janet Cooke was *pretending* to write a true story. My Times colleague wanted me to *pretend* to write a true story. Gail Sheehy, in her celebrated 1969 New York magazine story on "Redpants and Sugarman" — a prostitute and pimp who turned out to be composites, not real people — was *pretending* to write a true story. Granted, there may be 8-year-old heroin addicts *like* Jimmy and poker games *like* the one I could have created and hookers and pimps *like* "Redpants" and "Sugarman." But *like* isn't good enough for journalism.

I don't mean to sound old-fashioned or prissy or self-righteous — or like some sour old copy editor who only wants straight, boring, just-the-facts-ma'am, inverted-pyramid stories. Far from it. I realize that, especially in the age of television, newspaper stories must be vivid and compelling and innovative, or they won't be read. But newspaper stories also have to be honest, and I see no reason why a talented prose stylist cannot evoke drama or humor or pathos or whatever the subject requires, without simultaneously sacrificing honesty.

I am grateful to the "new journalists" of the 1960's for freeing us from the rigid forms of conventional newspaper feature-writing. I think they made it possible for many journalists to experiment with various styles that were previously limited to fiction. A good newspaper story can read like good fiction. Beginning, middle and end. Strong characters. Conflict. Suspense. Similarly, good narrative profiles can take a reader into the subject's home and heart and mind and soul — just as a good short story or novel does. But some liberties taken in the name of such experimentation blur the line between journalism and fiction, and when that happens, we risk losing our integrity and our credibility.

Truman Capote has described journalism as "a new art form ... the most underestimated, the least explored of literary mediums ... really the most avante-garde form of writing existent today." Well, yes. And no. The best of the "new journalism" — as practiced by Capote, Tom Wolfe, Gay Talese and others — has, indeed, been a new art form. Often, it has been brilliant. How many novels of the past generation have had the dramatic impact of *In Cold Blood*? But in the hands of lesser talents — of imitators more interested in sensationalism and celebrity than in either art *or* journalism — "new journalism" has been just another manifestation of the bastardization that has given us television docudramas in the name of pseudo-history.

"Roots." "Holocaust." "Washington: Behind Closed Doors." "Tail Gunner Joe." "The Trial of Lee Harvey Oswald." "The Missiles of October." All these (and many others like them) blended — blurred — fact and fiction. Can viewers distinguish between the two? Or will they see (and remember) these programs as more documentary than drama — as the ultimate truth about important (indeed transcendent) events in our history?

In *Executioner's Song,* Norman Mailer "scrupulously recreates every aspect" of the life of convicted murderer Gary Gilmore ... a "true tale ....A model of complete, precise and accurate reporting." That's what the book jacket says. But Mailer calls the book a "novel." Or, rather, "a true-life novel." Huh? Which is it? Truth or fiction? How is the reader to know? And how is the impressionable young reporter to react when he sees Mailer on all the talk shows and his book on the best-seller list and "Roots" on top of the ratings and other "new journalism" on magazine covers and newspaper front pages and theater marquees? What does that do to his commitment to verisimilitude — and to his appetite for fame and fortune?

Nine years ago, writing about "The Birth of the New Journalism," Tom Wolfe spoke of his astonishment at reading a Gay Talese profile of Joe Louis in 1962.

"It opened with the tone and mood of a short story," Wolfe wrote. This intimate, narrative approach seemed so much more characteristic of fiction than of journalism, Wolfe says, that his immediate reaction was, "What the hell is going on?"

As Wolfe read the piece, he says, "My instinctive, defensive reaction was that the man had ... winged it, made up the dialogue ....Christ, maybe he made up whole scenes, the unscrupulous geek...."

Talese had not made up anything. He had just written a marvelously sensitive and insightful and — at that time — unique journalistic profile. But other writers, trying to emulate Talese and Wolfe, have been less scrupulous. They do make up dialogue. And scenes. And blend reality and imagination — truth and fiction.

As John Hersey has said, "What began as the desirable process of applying the devices and modes of fiction to journalism has recently become something different. What's happened is that the heart of fiction itself — its sleight of hand — has been adopted as well."

Sleight of hand has no place in journalism.

A friend of mine recently sold a magazine story to the movies. He also sold the story to a book publisher. As a novel. I was puzzled when he told me the good news. "Was it a short story originally?" I asked him. "I thought I remembered it as nonfiction. Wasn't the couple you wrote about a real couple?"

"No," he said, "they were composites."

I tend not to like composites, but that's purely a personal preference on my part. Using composites seems lazy to me — cheating — like writing a dramatic, eye-catching lead based on a hypothetical situation and then saying, in the second or third paragraph, "This didn't happen, but it could have happened." I suppose, though, that if a composite is clearly identified as such, it's a perfectly legitimate technique.

"Was your couple described as a composite in the original magazine piece — in an editor's note or something?" I asked my friend.

He laughed.

"I just write the stories," he said. "I don't bother worrying about how the editors characterize them."

He damn well should worry about it — especially since his editors characterized his story, in a line above the title, as "A True-Life Adventure."

Does that really make any difference? I think so. I think a reader is entitled to know precisely what he's reading so he can judge it (and appreciate it) accordingly.

Teresa Carpenter of The Village Voice won a Pulitzer Prize for feature writing this year — the same prize that had originally been awarded to Janet Cooke. But one of the stories for which Carpenter was honored described the thoughts of — and contained statements by — Dennis Sweeney, the man accused of killing former Congressman Allard Lowenstein last year. Readers were left with the distinct impression that Carpenter had interviewed Sweeney. She hadn't. Ever. Why didn't she attribute her information then? "It's very cumbersome to say, 'According to sources close to Sweeney,' " she explained to The Wall Street Journal. It doesn't sound so cumbersome to me — unless the writer is more concerned with style than with substance, more committed to telling a good story than to relating facts.

Remember *Final Days*? Bob Woodward and Carl Bernstein, who had done a brilliant and courageous job of reporting for The Washington Post during the many months of Watergate, suddenly became not only rich and famous but omniscient, too. In their "moment by moment account of Richard Nixon's last days in public office," they seemed to know what people thought and felt and said at precise moments of specific days, even though neither reporter spoke to the primary party involved. Much — most, probably all — of what was in *Final Days* came from reliable sources. But how was the reader to know that? All interviews were conducted "on background," the authors said. There was virtually no attribution in the book. It read like a novel. A "true-life novel"?

Do journalism students and young reporters who read and admire Woodward and Bernstein (and Mailer and Talese and Capote and Wolfe) subsequently wonder, when they're writing their own stories: Why can't I reconstruct this conversation as it *probably* took place? And: What difference does it make if someone actually uttered the words I put into his mouth — especially if his name is changed (or withheld) — just so long as the essential truth of the story is there? And: What difference does it make if an event actually happened as I describe it, just so long as events *like* it happened and the issue involved, the cause, is important? What difference does it make if a few real characters (and one or two not-so-real characters) are combined into composites, just so long as they represent the kinds of people who could — no doubt, actually do — exist? Won't such a story have more impact, be more readable, reach more people?

In May, a talented young columnist for the New York Daily News was forced to resign to "save this newspaper from further embarrassment" after he was accused of having fabricated a story about a clash between a British army patrol and "a gang of youths" in Belfast. Although the columnist, Michael Daly, insisted his story was true, he admitted having used a pseudonym for his main source — without having acknowledged doing so in the course of his original story — and, when challenged, he said he could not substantiate his account with independent sources.

Daly's story from Belfast was filled with the kind of observations, direct quotes and detailed reports on dramatic, violent action that made it appear he was with the soldiers at the time the action (allegedly) took place. Certainly, Daly did nothing to dispel that impression for his readers. He wrote a vivid narrative account, unencumbered by such phrases as "eyewitnesses reported" or "he later said" or "one of the soldiers subsequently told me." But an investigation by the London Daily Mail failed to substantiate much of what Daly wrote, and the Mail called his story "a pack of lies . . . a work of pure imagination . . . a disgrace to journalism."

Daily News Editor Michael J. O'Neill lamented the "tragedy that so brilliant a career should be marred by this unfortunate incident" — and then accepted Daly's resignation.

". . . the credibility of this newspaper had to be given priority over all other considerations," O'Neill said.

Yes indeed. Credibility — more than news itself — is our stock in trade. An informative story is important. A dramatic story is desirable. An honest story is imperative.

DAVID SHAW, media writer for the Los Angeles Times, contributed this article to the July/August 1981 Bulletin.

On fictionalizing or faking facts

Tom Wolfe

I am amused by the current attempt to blame the Janet Cooke fiasco on some sort of new trend in journalism. Dream on. The "Jimmy's World" yarn was Old Journalism of vintage quality.

Every few years some newspaper writer is caught piping a story straight out of his skull, and this did not begin in the 1980's or the 1970's or the 1960's or, I dare say, the 1860's. It is an inevitable hazard of letting people near ink or Compugraphic consoles and blank paper and trusting in the good faith of what they write down.

When I arrived at the New York Herald Tribune in 1962, people were still talking about the great "Ship of Sin" scandal of Prohibition days. It seems the Trib had been informed that there was a ship operating off eastern Long Island, just beyond the three-mile limit, as a vice den of the high seas. The word was that this ship offered liquor, gambling and most known forms of sex. An investigative reporter (also nothing new) was sent out to find the floating fleshpot and board her and bring back the story. He was unable to find the ship, but he did find a saloon in Montauk, and he telephoned in a week's worth of the creamiest and most lurid chronicles in the annals of drunk newspapermen. The Trib couldn't print them fast enough. Half the city gasped; the other half headed for eastern Long Island to rent motor launches. When the hoax was revealed, the Trib fired the reporter, whereupon, legend has it, three other New York newspapers offered him jobs.

What makes the "Jimmy's World" case different is the fact that the story won a Pulitzer Prize. This is the first time a hoax has both won a Pulitzer Prize and been exposed, unless, of course, one counts *Roots*.

This is also the first time the press itself has felt compelled to moralize on the subject so earnestly. The reason is pretty obvious. Since Watergate, newspapers have made it their special mission to expose moral and ethical lapses among public officials, including the lightest of tiptoes down the primrose path, such as the assistant city manager's $120 lunch tab at the urban renewal conference in Denver. To be any less stern with their own sinners would not look upright.

The most convenient way out is to say that made-up stories are a new development in journalism, the ravages of a new microbe, some sort of Legionnaire's Disease of the ethics. How reassuring! All we have to do is isolate the bacterium and develop a prophylactic, such as the City Desk Anonymous Source Registry, and the problem is on the way to being solved.

No one — or no one I know of — condones the use of fiction in a newspaper except in the form of comic strips, serialized novels and pieces by those incredible lunatics who write for the Op-Ed pages. Nevertheless, I look forward to the spectacle of all the blimps in glen-plaid suits who will make speeches at the convention to tell the brethren that they don't condone it, either. It will be a considerable relief from the usual homily about "The People's Right to Know," which by now has hair growing out of its ears.

TOM WOLFE is the author of The Kandy-Kolored Tangerine-Flake Streamline Baby, The Pumphouse Gang, The Electric Kool-Aid Acid Test, The Right Stuff, *and* From Bauhaus to Our House.

Mike Royko

There's no reason for columnists to have a credibility problem if they follow the same simple rule that newspapers should follow. Not only newspapers, but the makers of canned soups, cars and any other consumer product. And that simple rule is to let the consumer know what he's getting. Truth in labeling, I guess it's called.

Good newspapers do it. The reader knows when he is getting hard news, an interpretive piece or an editorial.

And the good columnists do it. When I read Buchwald or Baker, I know I'm getting social or political satire. When I read Safire, Kilpatrick, Buckley, Kraft or Rowen, I know that I'm getting political opinion. The opinions might be dumb, but that's O.K. Saying dumb things is part of the columnist's craft.

The credibility problem arises when the reader doesn't know what he's getting from a columnist, or thinks he's getting one thing when he's getting another.

I think this is called "reconstruction." It means that the facts have been rearranged in order to make the story more dramatic, punchier and exciting to read. Sometimes it also makes the story a lie. That being the case, the word "faking" would be more accurate than the word "reconstruction."

There are many benefits in faking a story. It can turn a dull story into a vivid one. It can eliminate many gray areas and bring everything into sharp focus. It can make the readers gasp and marvel at the columnist's keen ear for dialogue and writing ability. It can make the columnist a star and make his paycheck bigger.

And if everyone on a newspaper did it, newspapers would be more fun than TV soap operas, and just about as accurate.

So the best approach for a columnist is not to fake a story. Or if he must, to at least include a precede that says, "The facts of this story have been rearranged to make it more exciting to read." Or "What you are getting here is not really what happened, but it's livelier this way, and it's the way I wish it had happened because it would more closely reflect my personal opinions."

Or maybe a simple bug that says, "Caution — this column is a fake. It could be hazardous to your knowledge."

MIKE ROYKO, a syndicated columnist of the Chicago Sun-Times, is the author of Boss: Richard J. Daley of Chicago.

Art Buchwald

I never met a columnist I didn't like. This is not to say that I never met a columnist I always believed.

My column is a little different from the others in that I start with a fact, and then go off and imagine what really happened or what could happen. I think I get away with it because I always plant a clue at the top of the piece to indicate that I'm making the rest of it up. This used to work but, unfortunately, nowadays the things that I make up in my head have apparently happened.

For example, on many occasions when I have written about the handling of some foreign problem by the State Department, someone holds a real State Department meeting and wants to know who leaked the story to me.

There are about three or four of us whose poetic license is accepted by the reading public, but the majority of columnists cannot get away with it. This doesn't mean there is not more truth in our columns than in theirs.

We also have the advantage that when someone doesn't agree with us he will say, "Oh, he was only kidding."

ART BUCHWALD is a syndicated columnist who appears in 500 newspapers. This article and the previous articles by Tom Wolfe and Mike Royko on faking or fictionalizing facts were published in the July/August 1981 Bulletin.

Bias still blights our newswriting

Lucille DeView

We've come a long way, newspersons, in raising the consciousness of our copy. Clearly we're fairer now than we were a short time ago, particularly in writing about race and the sexes.

But you don't have to read many newspapers to know we've still got a long way to go. . . .And that there are a lot of ways we can get ourselves into difficulty.

The Gray Panthers and several retirement groups prefer to be called older persons, not senior citizens. The disabled do not want to be called handicapped. The Eskimos (the word means "eaters of raw meat") want to be called Inuit ("the people").

Even as we rush to heal fresh wounds, however, we seem to insist on peeling off old scabs. A recent story told of "a park made just for drunks," not alcoholics. Another said: "She is a fiery Greek to his Swedish cool," hitting two ethnic stereotypes with one blow. And when one writer called Krishnas "zombies" and "ex-freaks," it caused considerable pain to one loving father of a Krishna follower who protested: "Cruel labels and all-purpose answers fall short of illumination."

Religion is an understandably sensitive area. When an editorial writer referred to the U.S. as a "Christian nation," a letter-writer said the phrase "offends, alienates and threatens me. As a Jew, I need a secular America, as do all non-Christians for whom America is home."

When the National Council of Churches recently announced an effort to produce a nonsexist translation of the Bible, many columnists treated the idea with anger or humor. "Utter rot," one said. "For Lord's sake! Feminists are rewriting Bible," a headline read. And there were guesses about changes in everything from the 23rd Psalm to wise men being called sages.

"The Bible can do without that kind of irresponsible speculation," said Edgar R. Trexler, editor of The Lutheran magazine. He reminded journalists that "after all, NCC produced the Revised Standard Version, which is a translation widely used by many who imagine the worst about the current project."

Most bias hides in assumption. "Rebecca is just one of the

guys" assumes junior high basketball will always be a male domain. Describing entertainer Hildegarde at one of her performances, at 74, as "remarkably active for her age and anything but senile," assumes weakness is the norm in the later years. It is not. Only 5 percent of all persons over 65 live in nursing homes, for example, though most stories about this age group are about this 5 percent.

A booklet, "Truth About Aging," published by the National Retired Teachers Association and American Association of Retired Persons, suggests not using these words and phrases which they say demean, patronize or stereotype older persons: cute, sweet, dear, little; frowning, feeble, fragile, gray, doddering; eccentric, obstinate, sad, senile; old maid, fuddy-duddy, Geritol generation, golden agers; stereotypes of older women as passive, dependent, frivolous, shrewish, nagging.

The booklet's statistics show that older persons enjoy active sports, sex, work, reasonably good health and citizenship. They dress well, and enjoy sociability not only with each other but with persons of all ages.

Many false assumptions are made about children. When one little boy, in a rare and tragic case, became a heroin addict, all youngsters were indicted by the headline, "Romper Room Junkies." And the preponderance of stories about troubled teens is seldom balanced with positive stories about their enormous courage and accomplishments.

Creeping bias is pernicious. It gets in our copy even when we mean to praise. Examples: "The articulate black professor" implies most black professors are inarticulate but this one is an exception. "The well-dressed Mexican children" implies most are poorly clothed.

We don't intentionally set out to commit bias. We are a caring profession. Our continual rush to deadline and need to be brief are partly to blame. It takes one less word to say, "Mary Jones, an epileptic," rather than "Mary Jones, who has epilepsy," though to Mary Jones, it's important to use the longer phrase because she does not want to be defined solely by her health.

In this International Year of the Disabled Person, we have an opportunity to bridge some gaps on behalf of people who do not see themselves as handicapped. They want to be independent and self-supporting; to be regarded as whole persons, not in the stereotyped, passive roles of the past.

Words to avoid: crippled (use impaired, limited, disabled, or be specific, as in paraplegic); crazy, insane, dull, half-witted (use mentally ill, retarded only when it is the correct description, developmentally disadvantaged, disabled or limited, or be specific); fits, spells (use seizures, epilepsy).

A fine story about a service for the hearing-impaired went awry when the headline called them "deaf and dumb." The editor, apologizing for this "terminology from the dark ages," told readers: "As editors and reporters, we ought to carefully consider the use of descriptive words and phrases that might be viewed as insensitive, or worse, pejorative."

We should also check photos for possible bias. A reporter who covered a protest at a welfare office brought back pictures of the leaders — two young, white mothers pushing babies in strollers as they picketed. The picture selected to run was from the photo files. It showed a black man in front of a welfare sign, this despite studies showing more whites than blacks on welfare, more young mothers than men.

One way to check for bias is to reverse the situation. Would we say: "Jerry Brown, noted white California governor...?" Why do we then continue to say: "Julian Bond, noted black Georgia legislator...?" If she is "one of the guys" in sports, is he "one of the girls" if he cooks or teaches small children? If the headline about Indira Gandhi's victory says "Woman of Destiny, Arranger of Flowers," under what conditions would we say of a male head of state, "Man of Destiny, Arranger of Flowers?"

Our own writers have much to say about bias. Richard Cohen in Washington, commenting on the unfairness of "divorcee," wrote: "It's code, newspaper code, if you like, like ruddy for drunk or jolly for fat....It's a statement about morals. 'Divorcee' means she ain't got none....But this is a standard we apply only to women."

Nickie McWhirter in Detroit, writing that "we revere bachelors, revile unmarried women," said words for single women — unmarried, bachelorette, spinster, divorcee, widow — have negative connotations not true of the word bachelor. Single? "To be single is to be alone. To be alone suggests loneliness or undesirability," she said.

I'm convinced the problem with bias is not with readers, who are often ahead of us in accepting change, but with ourselves. I heard an editor express outrage at the prospect of using "chairperson" instead of "chairman."

When The Washington Star discarded courtesy titles for women three years ago, few readers reacted. The same was true of several suburban Virginia and Maryland papers. Several small New England papers were the first to liberalize along nonsexist lines and heard little protest from generally conservative readers.

The Detroit Free Press, Los Angeles Times and The Boston Globe, among others, have more recently eliminated courtesy titles, something long advocated by the women's movement which points out there are no titles comparable to Miss or Mrs. to define the marital status of men.

The Free Press' new policy is designed to "treat the sexes in an evenhanded way, free of assumption and stereotypes." It calls upon writers and editors to avoid unwarranted physical descriptions; avoid sexist references; and eliminate demeaning stereotypes.

The New York Times, which persists in using courtesy titles, comes up with such inconsistencies in sports headlines as "Mrs. King Gains Quarterfinals, Borg Wins" and calls Nancy Lopez-Melton "Mrs. Melton."

Getting rid of bias does wonderful things for writing. When we can't lean on stereotypes, we are forced to make descriptions more accurate and individual. We put variety and vitality into our stories when we drop limited thinking and seek fresh sources — female surgeons, black doctors of adolescent medicine, female judges, all with expertise and ideas equal to their white male counterparts.

There are important stories to be written about children, the aged, race, religion, the sexes, the disabled. When we listen to people and respond to their concerns, we can do these stories with confidence and with words which help, not hurt.

We, of all the media, must be unbiased in our writing. We are the way-showers. Our newspapers come into homes. If we are respectful, decent, caring, loving, we can influence the language and ideas of others who will follow our lead. And that's what the world needs — now.

LUCILLE DeVIEW, who has conducted seminars on writing without bias for the Modern Media Institute and other organizations, currently freelances in Detroit. This article appeared in the May/June 1981 Bulletin.

Better be a
mother fudger

Theodore Bernstein

Jonathan, an 11-year-old nephew of mine, was held up by three other boys on his way home from school. He arrived home more excited than frightened and related the incident to his mother and his 9-year-old sister. "They took my wallet," he said, "and they called me a mother fucker." Whereupon 9-year-old Elizabeth interjected, "I didn't know you could fuck your mother." Jonathan turned on her contemptuously. "Didn't you ever hear of Oedipus, stupid?" he said.

This authentic, unembroidered story is related here because it opens up a few avenues leading to the heart of the troublesome problem of how the press should handle dirty words.

For one thing, I hope it demonstrates the jolting impact of such words in print, even in a publication addressed to a specialized and sophisticated readership. For another thing, it supports the argument, for whatever it is worth, that there is no point in making such words hush-hush since the kids know them all, anyway. For a third thing, it suggests that the youngsters are learning the vulgarisms at an earlier age than ever before. Surely, a good many of today's adults were not familiar with the four-letterisms when they were 9. And for a fourth thing, it brings out what is implicit, though not expressed, in the story: that today's mother, if she is inclined to be liberal, does not attempt to suppress the use of such terms lest by so doing she make them more enticing.

It may well be true that most children these days know the usually verboten words. But presumably they also know what the human form looks like and some of them may even have an idea of the ins and outs of coitus. Should they, then, be exposed to pictures of nudity and to open conversation about intercourse? And if so, why stop there? What about other bodily functions such as defecation and urination? Should they become a matter of public display and conversation?

No doubt there are parents who would answer these questions in the affirmative. "Let nothing be concealed," they would say, "and the world would be better off." But would it?

The something-withheld, the less-than-explicit has always

made art — whether it be the striptease or painting or poetry — more fascinating, more compelling, more powerful. It involves the beholder, enlisting him as a participant with the artist. Aside from art, the something-withheld is necessary for kindliness in human relations and effectiveness in political relations. Indeed, it can be persuasively argued that bringing everything out into the open would make the world coarser, crueler, less interesting and less operable.

The stress here has been on the young for a practical reason: The complaints about the use of obscenities in the mass media center chiefly on their effect on those who are growing up. Not exclusively, to be sure; many complaints also charge bad taste. But it is the young that the complainers seem to be principally worried about.

When you consider that television reaches all the youngsters and that newspapers reach a goodly number — considerably more than a tenth of the circulation of The New York Times, for example, is among students — the concern is understandable. The problem of television is much more difficult than that of the press since the broadcasting of vulgarities not only arouses viewers but also raises the peril of violation of federal law. But that is another question.

What course should the press follow when confronted with obscenities in news material? Editors are faced with the problem more and more urgently these days because of the widespread use of four-letterisms in riots, in campus demonstrations, in books, on the stage and in films.

The difficulty was posed acutely when the Walker commission issued its report last December on the demonstrations that accompanied the Democratic National Convention in Chicago last summer. The textual summary of the report, which was carried on the wires of The Associated Press, contained several instances of obscenities shouted during the disorders. Of such expletives Daniel Walker, director of the study team, wrote in a preface:

'We have, with considerable reluctance, included the actual obscenities used by participants — demonstrators and police alike. Extremely obscene language was a contributing factor to the violence described in this report, and its frequency and intensity were such that to omit it would inevitably understate the effect it had."

There can be no doubt, then, that the obscenities were an integral part of the news and of the report. Yet newspaper editors, after much knitting of brows, voted nay. Of 87 member papers checked by the A.P. only 14 used any of the text and only two — The Courier-Journal and The Times, sister papers in Louisville — included the vulgarisms. The other papers that printed any of the text used dashes, dots or asterisks. And even the Louisville papers regretted what they had done. As complaints poured in, Norman Isaacs, the executive editor, apologized and said, according to Time: "It was an error in news judgment. It isn't likely to happen again."

One of the troubles with printing obscene words in the press, no matter how compelling the reasons, is that the mere printing of them seems to give them a stamp of approval. In addition, there is the danger of setting a precedent: The reporter and the editor are likely to reason that, hell, we printed that word once so why not now?

We see four-letterisms in print all around us. *Portnoy's Complaint* is not atypical in the fiction field; it is fairly typical. Undergraduate newspapers are printing the obscenities and so are sophisticated weeklies like The Village Voice in New York. Then there are the new semiunderground sheets like Screw, Pleasure and The New York Review of Sex, which are devoted almost exclusively to vulgarity.

Why, then, does the daily press hold back? Simply because it is a mass medium. A person who buys the other publications knows, or should know, what he is buying; he is forewarned. He becomes a specialized reader. But the person who buys a newspaper buys it for quite different reasons. He has a right to believe that he can let any member of his family read it without being offended. The newspaper has an obligation to strike some kind of common denominator.

Incidentally, the failure to appreciate this distinction led the Columbia Journalism Review to speak unjustifiably, in the Winter issue, of "the apparent hyprocrisy of The New York Times, which deleted obscenity from the [Walker] text it printed on Dec. 2, but left it in the Bantam paperback edition that carries the paper's nameplate on the title page." The person who specifically buys the paperback book is a specialized reader quite different from the day-in-day-out purchaser of The Times.

There can be no doubt that the mores of the community are changing in the direction of greater liberality. A dozen or so years ago newspapers boggled at printing "hell" or "damn" or "goddam," but today there is no boggling. Where today you find "syphilis" and "gonorrhea," 20 years ago you would have found "venereal diseases" and 30 years ago only "social diseases." Each generation feels it has to draw the line somewhere. Unquestionably the line keeps advancing, still it has to be drawn. And the press would do well to hold back a little behind that line. If it insists on keeping up with it, it runs the risk of one day being left in an exposed position.

Whether we like it or not, the press is part of the Establishment, which because it is established is, in the most literal sense, conservative. And here an odd paradox is evident these days. On the one hand, the Establishment is the unwitting cause of much of today's anarchistic agitation, including the defiant reaching out for vulgarity. But on the other hand, the Establishment is the only visible bulwark against that anarchy.

Will the anarchistic trend continue? What is the outlook for the vulgarity revolution? Two trends seem possible. One would see the movement for bringing everything out of hiding continued and full exposure established permanently. The other would see the movement continued for a time, then halted by a swing of the pendulum or, to use the current word, a backlash. Of the two I would be inclined to put my money on the second.

Nudity in women's fashions is on the upswing at the moment, but fashion history tells us that similar developments have come and gone in Egypt, in Greece, in Rome and in France. There is no reason to expect such a vogue to be permanent here. Likewise, although sexual candor is prominent in the majority of today's movies, there are already signs of a reaction; I have heard more than one person say in effect, "I never thought I'd find sex boring, but these movies are getting me down."

And, as to four-letterisms, there is ample precedent for a backward swing. In only casual research I find at least half a dozen words — "arse," "fart," "piss," "prick," "shit" and "tit" — that were once standard English but now have been stuffed deeper under the covers. It is reasonable to expect that if they, along with the others, are dragged out into full daylight, they will thereafter be returned to their more accustomed places.

To be sure, some sordid words do achieve respectability and achieve it so completely that their shady backgrounds are largely forgotten. "Nuts," "bugger" and "bollixed" are in this category. But they are not the gutsy, elemental kind of words that have been under discussion here. The gutsy words, I would guess, will not remain out in the open for any extended period. But whether they do or do not, the newspaper editor has nothing to lose by being a little laggard.

THEODORE BERNSTEIN, author of Watch Your Language *and other books on writing, was assistant managing editor of The New York Times. This article appeared in the July 1969 Bulletin.*

Editing the writer

The conflict between writer and copy editor

Robert Phelps

One day in the early 1960's, Tony Lewis, then a reporter in the Washington Bureau of The New York Times, threw a temper tantrum, and with good cause. A copy editor in New York had changed "Ted Kennedy" in his article to "Theodore M. Kennedy" to conform to the newspaper's style of avoiding nicknames.

I was that copy editor.

A compassionate man, Tony forgave me, although I had been guilty of a cardinal sin of copy editing — writing an error into an article.

Moreover, I had contributed to the stereotype of copy editors as itchy-fingered incompetents who rejoice in butchering carefully crafted prose.

Who/what is a good copy editor?

Writers are remarkably in agreement in answering the question. They want someone who can spot errors but who checks with the writer before making changes. Curtis Wilkie of The Boston Globe, a stylist who has thrown more than a few temper tantrums of his own over senseless changes in his copy, puts his feelings this way:

"A good copy editor is one who gets back to the writer, who doesn't tinker with the lead without checking. I don't mind dealing with editors if they are good. They have made some damned good catches, but it doesn't make sense to tinker with my goddamned lead and not check with me."

Alan Richman, the assistant managing editor for writing at The Globe, adds to that idea:

"I'll tell you what I want in a copy editor. I want someone who is intelligent enough to spot mistakes and wise enough to allow me to make the corrections.

"If it is not possible for a copy editor to consult the writer before making corrections, or if the writer is too dense to understand what he did wrong, you need a much higher level of copy editor. You need one who knows how to write. I have found that 99 out of 100 copy editors know how to take a sentence apart and remove the offending part, but only one in 10 knows how to

82

put a sentence back together again. Nine out of 10 have no concept of style. They just know words."

My definition of a good copy editor is a bit more philosophic. A good copy editor should be somewhat of a paradox, possessing sympathy and hardheadedness at the same time. The ideal copy editor approaches the article with sympathy for what the writer is trying to do but is critical about the execution. The ideal copy editor does not fall into the common error of trying to shape the story the way he or she would write it. The copy editor assumes that the assignment editor has approved the general approach. (Of course, the editor does not blindly go ahead if someone had railroaded a piece that is overwhelmingly defective.) But the copy editor's first task is to attempt to make the approach work. In doing so, the editor is critical. Does the style fit the subject matter? Is the lead the best way to get into the story? Is the development orderly? Are there gaps in logic? Are there unanswered questions? Above all, are there errors in fact or violations of ethics or standards?

If the copy editor concludes that the story could be improved, he or she should go to the writer (or, if the newspaper's setup calls for it, the editor in charge of the writer) and suggest changes. If, after discussion, the writer disagrees, the copy editor should give in. After all, it's the writer's article. The only exception to this rule is that the editor should never permit a writer to violate a newspaper's standards or ethics.

Kenn Finkel, assistant sports editor of The New York Times, worked out a profile of an "almost perfect copy editor" while with The Miami News, Miami Herald and Newsday. This ideal copy editor has the broad academic background that comes from liberal arts, not from the usual journalism school. After college he shows a continuing interest in life by reading newspapers and books (fiction as well as nonfiction), traveling extensively, listening to good music, going to museums, following sports. The editor should also possess a certain skepticism that leads to an adversary relationship to the copy, but not to the writer. Obviously, the ideal copy editor needs to know grammar and spelling and should be fast and thorough. Extremely important, Finkel says, is that before going to the desk the copy editor work as a reporter. Finkel makes clear that he is not talking about a short stint as a writer. He means lots of writing for different departments — metro, national, living, sports — about many subjects. Only through writing himself can the editor get the broad view of what a reporter has to go through.

Finkel has also drawn a profile of the mix of copy editors for an ideal desk, firmly opposing filling it up with grizzled veterans waiting for retirement. Finkel likes six types:

Horses — These are the hard workers. They may lack finesse and style, but they can churn out the copy.

Wordsmiths — These are the stylists, those with a feel for words, who polish and tinker, until a story is a jewel. Electronic typesetting has given the wordsmiths the tool they need to edit and re-edit stories, playing with the copy in ways impossible with paper and pencil.

Fountains of Information — These are the editors filled with trivial and vital data on geography, politics, sociology and personalities so valuable in catching errors and filling gaps in articles.

Skeptics — These are the devil's advocates, those whose natural inclination seems to be to doubt everything, to ask millions of questions. They are a pain in the neck, but worth it.

Rewriters — These are the editors who can take information from six or seven sources and weave it into a well-organized routine 300-word article or the big story of 3,000 words.

Leaders — These are the men and women adept in the five skills, who can teach and guide the rim people. Every slot person should be a leader.

A copydesk staff like that would shatter the myth that rim people are introverts whose most daring form of recreation is to try the Twistagram instead of the crossword puzzle. (Anyone who has attended all-night parties at some copy editors' homes would never hold such myths.)

A copydesk like that would also go far to counter the undeniably widespread conflict between rim editors and reporters. Every office has seen it: the reporter who snarls at the questioning editor: "If you can't outwrite me, don't edit me." And the better response from the editor: "You couldn't write your way out of a chicken coop."

Alan Sutton, night editor in the sports department of the Chicago Tribune, believes copy editors suffer from a lack of recognition of their skills and responsibilities. He was ticked off by a Lou Grant episode portraying the frustrations of a deskman whose wife wanted him to write. That, Sutton said, perpetuates the feeling that the copydesk is a dead end.

Such talk, he noted, wounds the fragile psyche of copy editors and makes them hesitate before deciding whether to run the risk of questioning writers.

Roy Peter Clark, director of writing programs at the Modern Media Institute who says he has been less successful in working with copy editors than others, sees two reasons for the conflict. One reason is management's fault — the lack of a clear definition on many papers of a copy editor's role. How much authority does a copy editor have? Can a copy editor make significant changes, either with or without another editor's approval? Good management should make clear what the copy editor can and cannot do. "Everyone should know what his responsibility is," Clark said. The other reason is the writer's fault. Writers, Clark suggests, should thank copy editors who do good work. "Very rarely does the writer make that leap."

Clark is right. When the Italian liner Andrea Doria and the Swedish liner Stockholm collided on July 25, 1956, Max Frankel, then a rewriteman, wrote the lead story for The New York Times and I was his copy editor. A few days later Max put a package at my place on the National Desk. It was a bottle of gin.

"What's this for?" I asked.

"It's a tradition on the rewrite bank," Max explained. "When you win a publisher's prize you give your editor a bottle."

Hours later I learned that there was no such tradition. I told Max.

"Well," he said, "there ought to be one."

ROBERT PHELPS, assistant to the publisher and associate editor of The Boston Globe, wrote this article for the May/June 1981 Bulletin.

Developing and keeping writers

Don Murray

Newspaper editors across the country are attending and sponsoring writing seminars, hiring writing coaches, placing a new emphasis on writing. But it is not clear that the same editors really want writers in the city room.

I can understand why, for most writers are non-organizational men and women, self-absorbed, self-doubting, insecure to the point of false confidence, exceptionally sensitive to their own problems and insensitive to their editors' problems. But if editors want good writing in the paper they're going to have to nurture and support writers.

In the good old days — that really weren't so good — I became convinced there wasn't a place for a writer on a newspaper, even if he won a Pulitzer. I not only had a prize I also had a wife, a mortgage, a baby and plans for more. And once you were at scale the top salaries went to editors.

They wanted to make me an editor, but I wanted to be a writer. I didn't even want to become a columnist, for I'd seen writers who were given columns lose their legs and begin to have opinions. I wanted to be a general assignment reporter who covered news with a writer's eye. The publisher told me I was too highly paid — $140 a week — and had too many credentials to be a general assignment reporter. I left.

Now, 26 years later, I get paid more for a day of consulting about writing than I used to get paid for three weeks of writing (see what I mean?) and, as a consultant, I discover that many editors want to value writing without valuing writers. On most papers, the top salaries still go to editors and a few columnists.

Editors earn their pay. They have to deal with a flood of copy, much of it inaccurate, poorly organized and illiterate. Each edition of a newspaper is a miracle of executive decisiveness and editorial productivity, a refutation that Murphy's Law rules. Everything doesn't go wrong, just most things.

We need editors who can produce newspapers and also produce writers, editors who can tolerate, manipulate and support the self-indulgent, anxiety-ridden, half-child, half-infant people who turn out copy that isn't just up to standard, but is above and beyond newspaper standards. There are such editors, but to develop more we have to face some key issues. They include:

1. Respect. Listen to how editors talk to writers and about writers. You may hear some pretty surprising things. I heard an editor who was supposedly an expert on handling writers call the writers on his paper, "cocky pricks." I found that sexist, redundant and rather objectionable. I had no overwhelming urge to write for him.

Writers can be difficult people. I get bored by other writers whining. I even get bored by my own moaning. But the fact is that writing doesn't get easier with experience, for you constantly increase your own standards at the same time that you learn more and more ways to say the same thing. Increasing choice is the price the writer pays for success. Once the writer wrote the obvious lead, now a dozen leads are equally obvious.

The writer deserves respect and understanding for the challenges of this peculiar craft. You may learn to be an editor. I don't know about that, but I do know that you never learn to write, you're always learning, always vulnerable to flunking and being sent to the back of the room.

2. Tradition. I had forgotten how conservative most editors are. They may vote for liberals, but they live to enforce the traditions of journalism. Many editors seem to know precisely what stories, in what position, in what form and what style should be in tomorrow's newspaper.

Writers do not know. The best writers break through the cliches of vision; they see what they do not expect to see, hear themselves writing what they did not expect to write. Tradition to the writer is a challenge. The writer's goal is to be different; the editor's goal, too often, is to be the same. And that is exactly why newspapers need more writers.

3. Ego. H.L. Mencken said of the writer: "His over-powering impulse is to gyrate before his fellow man, flapping his wings and emitting defiant yells. This being forbidden by the police of all civilized countries, he takes it out by putting his yells on paper."

A writer's ego is like an unskulled brain, a quivering, unpleasant mass of vulnerability. Writers are exposed every time they write, and the more they write and the more their writing is praised the more terrified they become that they won't be able to do it again.

But editors should want that ego, for the writer with an ego cares, about what is said and how it is said. Editors should put up with and even encourage writers who care enough to make a commitment to a story. Reporters without egos who don't care how their stories are edited aren't writers — and they aren't usually very good reporters either.

4. Recognition. Editors can't command good writing, but they can learn to spot it. In the beginning the writer can be identified by as little as a word or a phrase, an approach or a voice.

This fragment of potential talent — the mastodon knuckle bone that tells an archeologist where one lived — is recognized by the feeling of surprise it inspires in the reader. The writer has produced a word or phrase or sentence that is both unusual and accurate.

Often the writer is unaware of this accident of talent, but when it is recognized by a skillful reader and not overpraised, but encouraged, the writer will begin to do what all good writers do, to take advantage of the surprises that clarify or reveal meaning and build effective writing from such unexpected moments of strength. Good writing does not result so much from the correction of error as from the extension of strength; we build on what works, and writers need help from editors to decide what works.

5. Praise. Writers are insatiable. Writers never grow to the point when they do not require praise. Give a writer one word of praise and the writer will roll over on the floor, tail wagging, feet in the air, saying give me more, more, more.

Editors shouldn't complain about this. Everyone has defenses against criticism, but no writer has any defense against praise. If you want to manipulate a writer, use praise. But if you want to manipulate a writer effectively, do not overuse general, patronizing praise — the ritual pat on the head — but give the writer a specific response that tells what you liked and why.

6. Limits. Creativity is not the product of freedom, but the product of the conflict between freedom and discipline. In an increasing number of city rooms I see good writers who are "rewarded" by removal of the usual limits of time and space. And I see writers who are spending weeks, and even months, on stories that should take time, but that much time? I'm also handed printouts to read that run 200 or 300 lines; sometimes those printouts even get into the paper, great unread tributes to the writer's status.

Writers may need more time and more space on a particular project, but that time and that space must be limited. It is the job of the editor to impose, in consultation with the writer, reasonable deadlines and reasonable limits on space, and then to enforce them.

7. *Distance.* The good writer often moves in close to the subject. The writer is involved, sympathetic and empathetic. One of the jobs of the editor is to help the writer achieve the appropriate distance from the subject. This isn't a matter of arbitrary formula — the distance necessary varies from story to story — but a process of discussion and focusing, so that the writer can be helped to see what the reader needs to know and feel and, perhaps even more important, what the reader does *not* need to know and feel.

The classic way to achieve distance was to insist on professional objectivity and hard news stereotypes. The result is poor, conventional writing.

The good writer will inevitably move in close and collect an abundance of interesting information. That is essential, for good writing is the result of selection, and what is excluded is, somehow, as important as what is included. There is a Zen saying, "To make a vase, you need both clay and the absence of clay."

It is the editor's challenge to help the writer discover the appropriate distance from the subject, so that the reader will experience the story. The writer needs the editor's help. Together they can take the essential step back, and from that distance see what needs to be left out — and left in.

8. *Power.* Some editors do not seem to realize the power they hold over writers. Even the most junior editor speaks for the institution and can summon the entire force of journalistic tradition to march against a single paragraph. The most senior writer starts at zero point on every story and always feels naked and alone before the editor, exposed by the draft which is being read.

Editors are armed with The Second Guess. They are upholding Standards. They are defending The Language against change. They are people who know what they don't want — after they see it.

Editors, of course, are sometimes almost as insecure as writers, and when an insecure editor meets an insecure writer it is a case of The Great Attack against The Great Defense.

Editors should try to feel secure in their power, to listen rather than command, consult rather than order. They have The Final Authority, and all writers know it.

9. Usage and Spelling. Of course, language must be used accurately and effectively. Of course, each word must be correctly spelled. Those are conditions of the craft, and they must be enforced. But, if editors only respond to usage and spelling, then writers feel that that is all editors value.

Our newspapers are filled with poorly written stories in which no grammatical rule is bent and no word misspelled.

If we want good writing we must value and pay attention to the entire process of writing, to collecting an abundance of specific information, to finding a focus that reveals meaning in that information, to developing a way of making the meaning clear to the reader and to removing every impediment to communication, whether it be a misspelling or an unnecessary detail, a graceless correct phrase or a graceful inaccurate one.

10. Absolute Rules. There aren't any. When I interview writers who are having serious problems writing and go over their copy with them, I find that they are giving their editors what they think their editors want.

The most irrational writing is often the result of rational acts. The writer is following principles the writer has been taught by an editor — or a professor.

I do not find lazy, stupid or rebellious writers. I find writers who are desperately trying to please their editors but who are applying inappropriate principles. They have been taught absolute rules about leads, attribution, quotes or a hundred other technical elements of newswriting and they apply those rules, rigidly. They catch hell, are given new rules and go back to repeat the cycle of anxiety and rigidity.

Editors have to find ways to encourage writers to make common sense decisions in a piece of writing by asking what the reader needs to know and the order in which the reader needs to know it.

11. Failure. All good writing is experimental, and every experiment has the potential for failure. If we play it safe, then there is no experiment. If editors want good writing, then they must support writers who have the courage and imagination to achieve large failures of vision, form and language.

The worst part of being a newspaper consultant is having to read edition after edition in which there are no large failures, just a predictable flow of uninteresting competence.

12. Time to Teach. I know that few editors feel they have the time to teach while they are under pressure to process a volume of copy that will achieve that minimum standard of accuracy and clarity I seem to deplore. I don't deplore it, but I hope editors will be able, perhaps, on just one story a day, to move beyond it. That takes time, but perhaps not as much time as we think.

We are teaching all the time, by attitude, by response, by lack of response. If we want better writing, then we must ask writers what stories they think should be written, and how they think they should be written. We must collaborate with them during the editing process, bring them into those meetings when news judgment is exercised, make them partners in the process of producing the paper.

Of course there isn't time to do this before each edition or on every story. But it is the responsibility of the editor to make the writer something more than a production worker, a laborer who is expected to produce for the foreman.

Collaboration can be achieved in minutes as well as hours. It's not so much a matter of time as attitude, a matter of asking rather than ordering and listening as well as speaking.

In our society respect often involves dollars, and newspapers that pay writers as well as editors might find that some of their best writers would come from the ranks of editors, who were once writers, but who were forced to become editors to survive. These born-again writers might, in fact, lead to a revival of writing on the newspaper.

Born-again or just born, newspaper editors must find new ways to develop and retain writers if they want writing to improve. I'm amused by the oldtimers who tell fond stories of editors who abused writers in the good old days. Those who tell the stories accepted the abuse and stayed. They don't mention the generations of young writers who received the abuse, chose not to become editors and left.

DONALD MURRAY, writing consultant and professor of English at the University of New Hampshire, contributed this article to the April 1981 Bulletin.

Wanted: more than a writing coach

Anthony Ripley

The solution to the problem of improving newswriting is not in the selection of a writing coach. Instead, it is a whole series of working attitudes and assumptions that revolve around how copy is gathered, written, edited, set in type and circulated to the public. The present system was put together to make newspapers accurate, clear, catchy and thorough (in part, those are definitions of good writing). The system is geared to take the worst copy from the office incompetent and make it readable. If good, creative writing comes through, it is a bonus. More often than not, the attempts by reporters to offer well-written pieces are discouraged by heavy-handed editing.

Few of the traditional writing and copy-handling methods of newspapers allow for writing improvement. But there is a deceptively simple answer: the creation of a super copy editor or super rewriteman to handle both problem stories. He works with the reporter but only for the editor on the desk, bypassing the usual copydesk flow so that the improvements are not undone by others. The reasoning works this way: It is clear, for example, that if a newspaper wants to improve the use and display of art, it must give the photo staff a much larger voice at a higher level in management. The same holds true for writing.

I will return to this concept later. First, I think it is important to examine newspaper attitudes. To simplify matters, the "city desk" stands for city, national, state or foreign desks. Let us start with a few general principles.

I. There must be a general atmosphere on the paper of reward rather than punishment. The person who tries to write a story or a head that falls short should be encouraged to try again, not damned for failure. This is the major problem at most American newspapers. Most editors feel that punishment is the best management technique. It works if you don't care about creativity or good writing. But that hard-boiled stuff is leftover mythology spread by newspaper romantics. Of course there are deadlines to be met and basic facts to be covered in any story. And these must be pulled together without a lot of handholding. But if we are trying to encourage writers and creativity, then the core is a fairly laid-back management which stresses encouragement, not recrimination.

II. Most of all, newspapers are dependent on their reporters — dependent to a remarkable extent. They are the paper's eyes and ears on the street. Most of the good copy — beyond routine assignments and reflex actions on breaking news — comes from reporters' instincts, contacts and enthusiasm. If the reporters are not out there doing for the management, then who is? Editors cannot think up all story leads and developments. And this, again, is why reporters should be encouraged, not punished.

What happens to reporters' copy is of great concern to each of them. In some newspapers, desks arbitrarily change copy as it comes in, never bothering to check with the reporter. But the reporter's name is on the copy when it appears in the paper. His reputation, his enthusiasm, his willingness to keep digging all depend on whether anyone on the paper is supporting him and paying careful attention to what he writes. Some of the most hideous arguments in any city room come over what some "butcher" has done to a piece of copy and the shame the reporter feels at having his name on an emasculated story.

Because of this, because of the need for accuracy and in line with "encourage, don't punish," editors should try to be sure that reporters are satisfied with the copy that appears under their names.

This concept is heresy to hard-liners on the papers. They feel, as befits junior-grade officers in any strict hierarchy, that they alone are revelators of truth and journalistic judgment for those below them. They may be for beginners. Their role with new staffers is that of a teacher. But any good deskman will tell you that a journeyman beat-reporter probably knows a good deal more about a story than the deskman does. And if the deskman begins meddling with his journeymen's stories without checking, he is digging holes filled with error and recrimination.

So it is not heresy to suggest that a reporter should be satisfied with a story that appears under his name. Anyway, editors will continue to direct operations of reporters, even if they do check story changes with the writers.

Put briefly, lead changes, substantive changes in the body of a story or large trims should be cleared with reporters when possible. This means the reporter should be reached — at home or wherever — for consultation. This requires those with a working story to leave a trail behind so they can be reached. That is no great organizational hassle.

III. Many of the problems in a city room lie with relations between the city desk and the copydesk. This will always be awkward and sensitive, because one desk is constantly substituting its judgment for the other's. It should be stressed that both sides should spend a lot of time defining their exact roles and duties. Both sides must recognize common goals. Also, the copyreader should be able to deal directly with the reporter when necessary without getting noses out of joint on the city desk or the news desk.

IV. All too often, copydesks are dumping grounds for failed reporters. This is a serious mistake. If a man is no good as a reporter, get rid of him or put him on midnight cops. But don't give the copydesk the idea that if they were any good they would be reporters. It is terribly destructive. Copyreaders should be encouraged to broaden themselves constantly. New copydesk hires should have areas of expertise, and slotmen should use those talents.

V. There must be time enough to consider stories instead of horsing them through. This means deadline rearrangements that allow more time on the city and copydesks. Again and again reporters will push close to deadlines, leaving the city and copydesks with almost indigestible lumps. So they quickly shovel through the pile and jam it through for a quick read and a quicker head. It leads to bad newspapers.

A good piece that can be improved with writing should be kicked around over a day or two or worked on between editions. Since the final edition is the showpiece of any morning paper (and the midday edition on the afternoons), most of the effort at good writing should be aimed at that edition. There is a natural desire to let sleeping dogs lie and not to meddle with the product once it is in type. This is a leftover from the old hot-lead days when change could be brutally expensive. But the VDTs, cold type and new printing plates make it cheap and simple to improve between editions.

The VDT is one of the real bonuses. A story can be in type in a few minutes so there is a huge cushion of time for improvement in the copy itself. It was almost 5 p.m. one afternoon at the Rocky Mountain News. Forty-seven stories were stuck in a jammed computer and there was a 7 p.m. deadline. But our computer people had all the stories in type by 5:45 p.m. — an unheard-of thing in the old hot-type days.

Circulation or composing will try to gobble up this extra hour or so that VDTs and computers allow. Fight for every minute. Give up as little as you can. It is one of the keys to improving the entire editorial product. It is time.

VI. There must exist a willingness on the part of all concerned to experiment with writing. We are all subjective judges and will tend to impose our personal views on each story passing through our hands. That does not mean our judgment is correct. The system of handling copy should be loose enough so that a reporter will try to extend himself — and loose enough so that an editor will be willing to gamble and run an experimental or creative piece about which he may have doubts. Copy editors should be willing to keep hands off a stylish story and not substitute a safe straight news story.

* * *

The above are general principles to encourage good writing and creativity. As for writing itself, the journalism books deal with that subject well. My own rules are borrowed from Arthur Brisbane, with some modifications:

1. See a thing clearly and describe it simply.

2. Keep in mind that the great crowd can't afford a corporation lawyer. But they can afford a 15-cent newspaper. You owe to the least of your readers the best and clearest explanation of what is going on. Your loyalty is to the public you serve.

3. Write your copy so that people feel they have actually seen what you describe.

4. Follow Tolstoy's rule in writing: "I don't tell; I don't explain. I show; I let my characters talk for me."

5. Use plain, simple English, striking English, even musical English. But avoid fancy phrases and, especially, avoid the mangled phrases of government. Develop a personal style and keep at it. Don't get silly avoiding the repetitious use of the same word, calling a dog a "four-footed beast, " a "canine," then a "woofer."

6. Avoid procedural writing. Don't write "The City Council Thursday night by a 6-3 vote amended City Ordinance 63-111. . ." when you mean,"If you spit in a public place it will cost you $100, the City Council ruled last night."

7. Feed your mind as you would your body, every day. Read everything you can get your hands on. But particularly read as much as you can of the best writers stressing history, philosophy, poetry, Shakespeare and the Bible.

8. Learn to edit your own copy. Keep it spare by throwing out

adjectives and adverbs if you can.

Remember that anyone in the press must do every day the work by which he or she lives, and then do it all over again the next day. Each day you create your reputation anew. Your greatest asset is enthusiasm, real interest in what you see and tell. The years are the enemies of enthusiasm. When you feel it ebbing in you, look for other work.

With these things in mind, let me get back to the super copy editor or super rewriteman. In some papers, he is given the title of Associate Managing Editor and has final say over writing from the city, state, national and foreign desks. A man can be installed there or at the right hand of each of the editors. To find the right people, break loose a likely-looking rewriteman or copyreader and give him the special assignment for writing. Leave him on the rim or at the rewrite desk, if you wish. That way losers can melt back to their old jobs without problems.

An outside coach can come in and, for a time, have a very real effect on writing, because he is beyond the present power structure of the newspaper. But once he is gone, his influence will dwindle. The real secret to better writing is a full-scale commitment on the part of management. That means creating internal coaches with authority, and that means a system that encourages reporters and deskmen instead of punishing them.

All these pieces fit together. The solution is not some outside, visiting star, but in ourselves.

ANTHONY RIPLEY, managing editor of Denver's Rocky Mountain News at the time he wrote this article, is director of congressional relations for United Way of America. The article, which first appeared in the Minneapolis Tribune, was published in the September 1978 Bulletin.

How to achieve peace with the copydesk

Alexander Cruden

On a bulletin board in the reporters' area of the Detroit Free Press newsroom is this unattributed quotation:

"The headiest drive in the world is not love's orgasm, or hate's dagger, but one man's need to change another man's copy."

Reporters say the only progress journalism is making in this regard consists of opening the way for women to change copy, and have theirs changed.

"If I don't change the copy," responds the copy editor, "why am I here?"

Lives there a journalist who hasn't been, at some point, passionately on one side of this attitudinal battlefield?

It may be easier for those who have been on both sides to reach truce terms, to bring productive peace to the newsroom. A truce is essential. Without trust in each other's crafts, reporters and copy editors wage spiteful skirmishes in which the copy — the readers' interest — is the chief casualty.

We'll list five methods of arriving at this treaty. In fact, we'll discover one central truth: In principle there is no conflict, and the key to making that a practical reality lies in developing professionally self-confident copy editors.

1. Make room for the individual.

When asked what was the most interesting thing they read this week, most copy editors are likely to cite the story that was most unusual. Yet, in practice, too often they tend to apply guidelines as rules and turn the unusual — phrase, story structure, tone — into the mundane.

Whatever explanation the copy editor gives for making the change, in almost every case the motive is "I was trying to do my job."

The copy editors' supervisor needs to build from there, starting with the slot.

The slot editor should be not only an ace grammarian with first-rate news judgment, but a positive-spirited soul who cherishes the specifics which make one story different from another, and who imparts that love of details to the rim.

In the same way, the slot editor should convey the expectation that some of the newspaper's rules of style will be set aside on occasion, not through ignorance but for some higher purpose — which is open to discussion.

2. *Let there be consistent accountability.*

Every mistake in the newspaper was made by somebody, and we should fire the copy editor who is to blame, the reporter suggests. "I fixed 499 things and missed one," the copy editor responds, "and guess which decision in 500 I hear about."

Supervising editors need to be judicious in deciding which mistakes to make a case of. These guidelines have been found helpful:

a. Don't have the reporter take it up directly with the copy editor after the fact. The time for these two to discuss the story (or even the headline) is when they can improve the copy, before publication.

b. Reporters' questions should go to the copy editors' department head. The supervisor may have dealt already with the problem, or may know of other relevant factors.

c. The supervisor may want to check with the slot editor before going to the rim, or check the slot's work on the story, for that may be where the error was born. On the other hand, the slot editor may have noticed a pattern of mistakes by a rim editor, something the supervisor should deal with on a larger scale.

d. Gentleness is often appropriate, keeping in mind that 499-1 proportion in the copy editor's experience.

e. It's usually more fruitful to discuss why a copy editor made a change that hurt a story (the change that causes next morning's reportorial screams) than why the editor overlooked an existing error. Ideally, this discussion allows the editor to see how to improve professionally, at least in some small degree, and should help bring home the real-world importance of what copy editors do.

f. It helps to let reporters know that a complaint was pursued. Of course an error-free future cannot be promised, but reporters are much less inclined toward continual harping at the desk if they know serious complaints are seriously followed through.

(There was a time at the Free Press when one top-flight reporter lost all regard for the integrity of the copy flow. A series of apparently capricious alterations in his prose went unaccounted for. The final indignity came when he quoted a Biblical verse — and picked up the next morning's paper to find even that was changed. In defense of copy editors, it must be pointed out that eventually it was discovered that a zealot in the composing room had taken it upon himself to change Holy Writ.)

3. Let there be praise, too.

Copy editors need to have more positive goals than simply the absence of error.

Newspapers have come up with systematic rewards, offer cash for the best headlines of the week, month or year. Some publish in-house critiques, full of compliments as well as carping. One excellent guideline, as practiced at The Miami Herald in Jerry Ceppos' Slithy Toves, among other critiques, is to print names only when individuals are being praised. The errant among the staff can mend their ways anonymously.

Another commendable practice is to cite good copy editing itself, not just the easy-to-spot fine head.

In this regard, newspapers might well consider honoring the appropriate copy editors when its reporters win journalism prizes.

An informed pat-on-the-back from the boss never hurts either.

4. Challenge the writing, not the writer.

A certain byline will trigger a set of error expectations in the experienced copy editor. One mistake-prone film critic, for instance, as often as not even got the name of the movie wrong, yet she'd complain vituperatively about wrongs (real and imagined) committed to her copy. Was this taken personally by the copy editors? Well, yes.

On the other hand, if supervisors — particularly the slot editors — can enlist the rim editors in a kind of resilient camaraderie, an attitude that says we can take whatever you dish out and, in fact, improve it, the personal sniping can wither away.

If the copy editor can measure pride in the degree of improvement, rather than in the number of mistakes fixed, the staff is on its way to empathy.

5. Consider the job switch.

Some newspapers have found former copy editors are among their best reporters, and vice versa. Very few go about cross-education systematically.

One ambitious project was begun recently by Managing Editor/Daily Tim Leland at The Boston Globe. It has two parts.

Under the "Writer-in-Residence" program, copy editors volunteer to be reporters for two-week stints. Each usually chooses a particular story angle or series. A copy editor can do this any number of times, the desk's workload permitting. Simultaneously, the copy editors (as well as regular reporters) work with a writing coach, an assistant managing editor assigned to improve The Globe's words.

The other part of Leland's approach is "Editor for a Day." The complexities of VDT copy editing prevent reporters from taking a quick dip on the desk. So instead each spends a day observing the production process, spending a lot of the day watching how and why editors make decisions and what it takes in the back shops to produce the paper.

The project is too new to evaluate, but Leland says the immediate response was positive.

It began, he says, with "a feeling that copydesk people . . . too often don't have sufficient variety in their work . . . and reporters do a better job if they understand the other side of newspaper production."

Now, Leland says, "each side gets to know the other's problems" as well as "an opportunity to stretch their minds."

Mike Cooney, copy editing supervisor at the Minneapolis Tribune, has seen the job switch fail. More often than not, he finds, reporters on the copydesk are "more trouble than they're worth." But desk people at the Tribune do get a chance to write and report from time to time.

At the Louisville Courier-Journal, individual reporters and copy editors work on the other side of the story on an irregular basis, for six months at a time.

John MacDonald, Courier-Journal national editor, says the process helps reporters "develop some degree of confidence" in the desk, and editors come to understand that reporters "don't just have stories fall in their laps."

He thinks the six-month stint gives reporters the necessary time to become proficient on the editing keyboard and editors the time to do some substantial reporting.

In addition, MacDonald teams copy editors on a sustained basis with reporters once a major story project is under way.

In a similar vein, a new program in the Detroit Free Press newsroom matches individual copy editors with areas covered by the paper's foreign correspondents.

These desk editors do the final editing and heads on correspondents' and related wire service copy, put together background pieces from wire and news library resources and suggest story ideas and contacts to the national editor, who remains the correspondents' chief editor.

And in sum...

As Dave Lawrence, executive editor of the Free Press, puts it, the goal is to "get everybody moving in the same direction." In particular, each copy editor should feel a positive involvement in the paper's quality.

To come to peace terms with the reporting side, the copy editor becomes not a cutter, but a finisher; a builder, not a demolitions expert.

Without reporters there are no stories; without imperfect reporters there are no copy editors.

ALEXANDER CRUDEN, formerly copy editor, assistant city editor and assistant to the managing editor, serves as national/foreign editor at the Detroit Free Press. He wrote this article for the May/June 1981 Bulletin.

What do young writers seek from an editor?

Tony Schwartz

Asking a young reporter to come up with a model for the ideal editor is a little like requesting a teenager to describe the ingredients for a perfect set of parents. It's a nifty fantasy, but acting on it suggests a conceit that hasn't really been earned.

From this curious dilemma emerges my first rule for the ideal editor: Trust the reporter's instincts entirely. If he resists an assignment, simply nod agreeably and offer him complete license to write whatever he wants, at the length he chooses, on his own schedule. And then print the story as written.

Actually, that isn't my fantasy at all, and I think it's fair to say that most young reporters would much prefer to work with an incisive editor than with one who never makes a mark on a story or ventures a suggestion for improving it. But just what are the qualities that the reporters I know most appreciate and respond to in an editor?

For me, the ideal editor combines a rare and delicately balanced set of qualities: the capacity to be both encouraging and critical, a willingness to give reporters freedom but also to establish boundaries and the desire to create an atmosphere of mutual trust and respect, rather than one that is more distant and rigidly hierarchal.

Above all, perhaps, it helps a reporter to work primarily with one editor, or at least with one editor who plays a supervisory role. That isn't always possible on a large newspaper but the advantages are numerous. An editor who works regularly with a reporter is more likely to get a sense of that reporter's rhythms, strengths and shortcomings, and to be sensitive to them. I feel best when I sense that I have access to my editor, that the editing process is not an adversary proceeding that begins only after the story is written.

Frequently, I find it valuable to discuss a story with an editor midway through my reporting, or my writing, if for no other reason than to have a sounding board for ideas. I've worked in rigid setups where one editor assigns the story, another edits it and no discussion is expected in between. One of the resulting problems, I think, is that the reporter feels less comfortable about letting a story evolve if the reporting dictates changes in the original idea. The reporter also loses the advantage of having the sort of input that might keep a story on track when it is threatening to go off.

Trust is essential to a good working relationship between reporter and editor, and it needs to be mutual. The editing of stories is obviously the most sensitive subject between reporter and editor. The editor who derives his satisfaction from helping a reporter improve his stories while maintaining the reporter's voice is much more likely to inspire a sense of trust than the editor who simply works on a finished story without regard for the reporter. There is a huge difference between an editor who tells a reporter, supportively, "You can do better than this" and the one who says, simply by his actions, "I can do better than you."

Clearly, an editor can play a variety of roles, from assigning the story, to helping structure it, to making suggestions about omissions, to doing the line-by-line editing. To me — and I'm sure other reporters have other priorities — there is nothing so dispiriting as the editor who tries to improve one of my pieces by rewriting it. I don't mean to suggest that I'm churning out flawless stories day in and day out, but I find that I learn more, and that I come out of the experience with a better feeling if an editor suggests problems and lets me make the changes. If an editor points out that a paragraph I've written is too flowery, or that the story lacks a setup, and permits me to do the work, I feel as if the story remains mine.

When an editor substitutes his own language, or adds a whole new paragraph for clarification, I think almost invariably the reporter comes away with a sense that the rhythm of the writing has been altered, and that the story is not so much a personal project. I'd argue that any young reporter cares almost as much that a story retains his style, as he does about having a byline. If editors want to encourage good writing, it seems to me critical that they give reporters the freedom to evolve individual voices, even if that means indulging some awkwardness along the way.

Finally, I believe that the best editors are those who play to the individual strengths of their reporters, rather than treating everyone equally and democratically. Reporters have varying qualities, and it is rare that any reporter does everything equally well. Certainly, there is something to be said for encouraging young reporters to stretch themselves, and do a variety of kinds of pieces. But the sorting out process doesn't take long to occur. There are some reporters who write clearly and accurately on tough deadlines, but simply don't have the instinct for longer profiles. There are others who write slowly but stylishly, but simply can't pull together a spot news story efficiently.

Some editors might say that making choices in the way that I'm suggesting creates resentment on the staff. Perhaps that does occur. But I'd say that in the long run, it pays off. Almost any reporter wants to feel unique, chosen for an assignment not just because he is available at that moment, but because he can bring something special to the assignment. And the happiest and most effective reporters are invariably those who are encouraged to tap their strengths and strut their stuff.

TONY SCHWARTZ, who covers the television beat for The New York Times, wrote this article for the April 1981 Bulletin.

Sportswriting

The prose of sportswriting

Bob Broeg

Sportswriting has gone from verse to worse, which really isn't right or even correct. But it has changed from purple prose with paeans to almost complete locker-room coverage in which what the athletes say has replaced what they do.

Oh, somewhere in this promised land is a compromise. We don't want those overwritten flowery pieces preceded often by rhymes or limericks. Nor do we need to be told again and again and again, so help me FDR, that this batter was said by that pitcher to have hit a hanging curve or that the line in front of the bull-necked back opened gates big enough — in the grateful ball-carrier's view — to run the entire student body through.

In the past, before I began to write professionally and even afterward, sportswriters dropped the word "courage" into stories as if they were writing medal inscriptions. The truth is, World War II cooled off that kind of label for athletic endeavors. Now, by contrast, there's a tendency to a smart-aleck approach or reproach.

Somewhere between the period when the press rarely invaded the clubhouse and now when they would like to take typewriters or electronic terminals there, we've gone from too little reaction from the athletes to too much. From not quoted enough, the guys and gals now are quoted too often. Obviously, from the retreat of so many into silence, they don't like it.

As a writer, I don't like it when a player or coach or manager won't answer a short, direct question. Especially those intended to straighten out me and, hopefully, to clarify things for the reader's benefit. As a reader, I don't like it when a writer won't analyze for me what he has seen or felt, but, instead, falls back on the self-serving platitudes or attitudes of the players.

Now, honestly, I don't think there's enough literary change of pace. Even with the intrusion of radio and television, a good old-fashioned narrative — written with the skill of a guy who knows damn well he could recapture the Johnstown flood or the Hindenburg crash if given the chance — works to make a key play or situation come alive for the reader. Yeah, even the reader who might have seen the game or heard it or watched it.

A writer who has learned his game, who has looked and listened day after day, should be able to review a sport with the confidence of a drama or movie critic. Why not use quotes when they're really meaningful, when they expand or explain what happened?

Obviously, in the need to compete, editors encourage the controversial to the point that some reporters who don't know a furlong from a fetlock, or a love set from a love seat, are making literary wild pitches. These DO infuriate athletes, believe me.

At times, writers past hero-worshipped. Now, they denigrate. Certainly, sports action has become inaction, passing from the athletic court to the locker room and courtroom. And, from jock-strap itch to the strapped-for-salary hassle.

In 1958, a wordmaster, J. Roy Stockton, who had caught the flair and flare of the colorful Gas House Gang with an eye and ear for amusement, retired as sports editor of the Post-Dispatch. He turned over the toga to me with these words:

"I'm tired of having to be a doctor and a lawyer even more than a reporter or writer."

Uh-huh, 22 years ago! All that needs to be added to JRS' comment is the word "agent" and he'd be as up to date as tomorrow's pitchers or the weekend football betting odds.

Actually, I believe writing is better now. More writers write well. It's more succinct, even though I don't qualify for that classification. I believe reporting lags. I think there's a tendency too often to avoid detail.

Personally, I believe it's possible, whether writing first day or second, to combine human interest, observation and commentary with enough information to satisfy any reader.

Above all, dammit, I believe it's essential to be able to write from a different stance, as dictated by what your heart and head tell you, not by a format that calls for either too much or too little reliance on what is said by the athlete or the person who theoretically tells him what to do.

If the prose of old was too fat, now it's almost too lean. If there was one time too much gee-whiz writing, now there's too much of an aw-nuts approach.

As one who thinks sports essentially belong on the sports pages, not page one — meaning that I don't want to overemphasize the Fun and Games Dept. — I believe sports ARE the country's greatest common denominator this side of the last inhale and exhale. Sports competition helps many people blow steam.

It's a relief for those with enough personal reasons to seek a psychiatrist's couch. I believe the average bloke wants to use sports to forget if not forgive. Above all, when the reader kicks off his shoes and turns to the sports section, I believe, he wants to be entertained more than informed and informed more than infuriated.

Maybe I'm wrong, but, as one who likes to write more about persons than teams, places or things, I believe readers like to read mostly about other people. And even though I think we're beholden to treat the silent player objectively, it IS nice to be able to get the quote or two you DO need or want.

The art of it, as I see it, is to be able to write with the integrity and skill that will enable you to retain a rapport with athlete and management without giving either the feeling that you're pro-boss or pro-player.

If neither side is pleased, maybe you've done your job best of all.

BOB BROEG, sports editor and assistant to the publisher of the St. Louis Post-Dispatch, wrote this article for the November 1980 Bulletin.

Five principles of sports punditry

Leonard Koppett

Writing a column about writing a sports column is an excellent example of something to avoid. Going ahead with something one would like to avoid is an excellent example of what daily newspaper production requires. So here we are.

The trouble with writing about writing is that almost anything you say turns out to be self-evident (to those who can write), or incomprehensible (to those who can't) or simply slick.

All this is especially true of writing a sports column, but a discussion is worthwhile nonetheless. In daily newspapers, the sports column appears in greater volume than any other single type of column. It is attempted by more individuals, with less direction and attentive editing, than anything else that is permitted comparable editorial freedom. Yet those who read it, on the average, know more about the subject — or are convinced they know more — than the readers of other parts of the paper.

There are, then, some truisms — not rules, but evidence accumulated by observation — that can be stated.

With respect to the writer, the first consideration is personality. Over a period personality will come through whether the writer likes it or not. It cannot be concealed or falsified. The whole point of a signed column, with or without mug shot attached, is that the reader identifies the columnist as a specific person — knowledgeable, witty, profound, stupid, insufferable or illiterate, as the case may be in any particular reader's opinion, but specific.

Therefore, it's essential for the columnist to be himself or herself. A stock situation in sports literature is the champion, idolized by the public with a press-created image, who really is a jerk. Or, there is the gruff-exterior coach whose inner kindness is not recognized by the outside world. Frequently there is truth behind this stereotype of image-reversal, but that can't happen to a columnist. Anyone who expresses a viewpoint daily in print reveals personality as surely as on a psychiatrist's couch.

An attractive person may not, for countless reasons, be able to produce an attractive column, but a dull one will certainly produce dull columns.

That word, "viewpoint," which slipped in a couple of paragraphs back, is the second key. It is quite different from "opinion," which has only a limited place in writing a column — of any kind.

A viewpoint is an angle of vision. It is the unifying force for the insights, descriptions, reports, conversations, analyses or jokes the columnist offers the reader. It should be consistent over time (which is why the writer's personality is so important) and identifiable.

Switch, for a moment, to the position of the reader. The sports section is the part of the paper that contains news with entertainment content, as distinct from just news (main section), just entertainment (comics and features) or news about entertainment (drama and music). Sports news is entertainment and news welded together.

In that section, the columnist is the reader's particular friend (or enemy). He's the guy you argue with at the bar, or the buddy you go to the game with, or that idiot Dodger fan down the block, or a respected teacher. The columnist's advantage is that he can be where the reader can't, and accumulate lore the reader couldn't get for himself. Still, unless the reader feels comfortable with the columnist's established and identifiable viewpoint, there will be no basis for the special relationship.

The reader turns to the news, features and box scores to find out what's going on. He turns to the columnist to see what the columnist has to say about what's going on.

But if the viewpoint is going to illuminate anything, and keep the reader's attention (to get back to the position of the writer), the columnist must have valid and abundant raw material. He has to make use of the advantage the reader counts on — that the columnist can be *there*. So a columnist must be an active information-gatherer, much more conscientiously than a beat reporter. He doesn't, of course, go as deeply into the daily affair of one subject, as a traveling baseball writer would, but he has to be familiar with and familiar to all the major sports activities in his area and nationally.

Finally, both writer and editor must accept the fact of life that no one bats 1.000, or even .500. No columnist is going to be brilliant five days a week; two would be terrific. The true goal should be consistent satisfaction, not an occasional dazzler. The reader invests his 10 minutes or so to read the column and deserves a fair shake every time, so the first responsibility is to minimize "bad" columns. And what usually makes a bad sports column is the columnist's failure to hustle, to get worthwhile material rather than retreat to rhetoric·or a gimmick.

If you've come this far, you can see why I don't think "style" needs much discussion. Style emerges from the writer's personality and activity. (Naturally, if the person had no facility at all with language, you wouldn't have him writing columns in the first place.) But because personality and viewpoint are paramount, the worst thing a columnist can do is to try, consciously, to imitate another's style.

There are hundreds of "good" styles, just as there are hundreds of personality types, and countless circumstances. My definition of "good' is "appropriate." Jim Murray's one-liners, Red Smith's polish, Dave Anderson's eclecticism and, in an earlier time, Jimmy Cannon's imagination. Grantland Rice's romanticism or John Kieran's erudition are not models to follow but techniques to be learned and absorbed into one's own honest expressions. And they become useful techniques only when (and if) they are fully absorbed, not copied, and applied at the proper time to the appropriate subject matter.

In light of all the aforementioned, there seem to me to be certain preferable principles, preferable for no better reason than that they seem to give satisfaction over the years. These include:

1. A "fun-and-games" attitude is better than "life and death."

2. Good grammar is better than runaway colloquialism.

3. One topic per column, well treated, is preferable to tying together different themes or touching all bases at some major event — although good "notes" columns, from time to time, are the best thing in any sports section.

4. Writing about other writers or broadcasters, or about one's own gripes, hardships, conflicts or dislikes, stinks.

5. A pedestrian column about something is better than a deeply-felt literary tour de force about nothing.

And keep it within the allotted space.

LEONARD KOPPETT, executive sports editor and columnist for the Peninsula Times Tribune, Palo Alto, Calif., also writes a weekly column for The Sporting News. This article appeared in the November 1981 Bulletin.

An interview with the dean of sportswriting

Jim Murray

QUESTION: How do you start writing a column?

MURRAY: Basically, I figure that any writing, long or short, has got a beginning, middle and end. And is about a person rather than a thing. I rarely write about things. I don't think people care about things. I think people care a little bit about money, but I don't think they care about most other things.

When I was working for Time, we had a guy who was a very scientific, Germanic type. Typically, he was all excited about this new method of stamping out fuselages, you know. And he kept bringing this story in, telling about how many valves went in it and all that. And, I said, "Jesus, John, readers out there don't care about that." And he says, "Well, what am I going to do? It's about a new method of stamping out fuselages." And I said, "Can't you go find the little old professor who thought of it? A guy who swears, is absentminded and has dandruff on his collar?" I says, "You can start off with him and then you can bring your damn fuselage in."

And I've always held to that. You can inform people if you tell it through characters or situations. Well, David, you know what I'm talking about. Right from the start I took the attitude that, one, people are interested in people; two, I won't just write down "RBI," because women won't know it means "run batted in." So I explain it. Those are the things I try to do in writing a column.

QUESTION: And those things have sustained you through two decades?

MURRAY: They've had to. I'm not getting any smarter.

QUESTION: How do you get up for the task every day for 20 years? How many columns do you write a week?

MURRAY: Well, I wrote six originally. Then I went to five, but at the time I was reluctant because, you know, if you write six you can afford two pieces of garbage. If you write five, all of a sudden you want to make every one like the Lord's Prayer on the head of the pin.

Then I got very comfortable and then I lost my eyesight. And it was a struggle to do three. When I regained partial sight, then I said I'd go back to four. So I've done thousands of them — six a week for I don't know how many years, five a week for most of my life, three and four a week the last year and a half.

QUESTION: Do they all start running together?

MURRAY: I try very hard not to repeat myself. I've had a couple of books of collections of columns. Sometimes, when I suspect I am repeating myself, I take a peek. And it makes me angry, because I figure the reader wouldn't remember, anyway. But I try not to have it all run together.

Sometimes, when you're on a frantic thing like a World Series, Super Bowl or a big fight, you tend to write the column and you dream about it all night.

For years what I did was go interview a guy and I'd let the column kind of ferment over night. But you can't always do that. One thing is for sure — I've never found a column that writes itself.

QUESTION: Your style is distinctive. You're great at humor. How did it evolve?

MURRAY: When I was with Time magazine, the style they used to have was terse. It was amusing. They would strive to compress facts and details. I remember when Hubert Humphrey first went to Washington, when he first got elected to the Senate, I had only 10 or 12 lines and spent the day trying to fit everything in. Anyway, I think all that training had an effect on my writing style, made it easier for me to write the column.

I've only been writing the column for 20 years, by the way. Red Smith has been at it for 50.

When I first started writing the column all of a sudden I had 680 words. This seemed like a lot, given my experiences in the old days at Time.

QUESTION: Do you still write 680 words?

MURRAY: No, it got to the point where I used to be two columns wide and two full columns deep on the left side of the sports page, and I would bring it to a screeching halt rather than have it jump to another page.

But I had the whole 680 words. Then they went to the different makeup, six columns rather than an eight-column page, and I was compressed to where the column looked like it was 90 percent hyphens. At that point I said to hell with it. I'd probably have to write 609 words and they would all be hyphenated. I went to the bosses to take the picture of me out so I could have more words in. They did take the picture out, but they still jumped it. I don't write the kind of a column that a guy can take scissors and clip the bottom of it. Because usually my last paragraph ties up the whole thing, or puts some kind of little ribbon on it, you know? And so I began to jump. You can't avoid a jump the way the makeup is going in newspapers these days. Everybody jumps now.

QUESTION: Do you have any idea how long you write anymore?

MURRAY: No. Yeah. Oh, sure I do. I keep it in two pages of ordinary paper.

QUESTION: Two pages of 8 x 11-inch paper?

MURRAY: Yeah.

QUESTION: Double-spaced?

MURRAY: Yeah.

QUESTION: Wow, that could end my career!

MURRAY: Why?

QUESTION: That's short!

How do you maintain your enthusiasm for writing a column? For writing sports four times a week?

MURRAY: Well, I need the money. That's a great motivator, David.

My feeling is that writing is writing. I think I know that better than someone who's been in sports all his life, or even most of his life. Because I spent — let's figure it out. . .well, in 1941 I was a college correspondent. So I began writing then. And I spent 20 years on other kinds of writing. Oh, I had five years doing sports for Sports Illustrated. And I find that writing is writing whether the story is about Maury Wills or about George Bush.

You're still required to talk to the guy, to try to describe him to the public. And that's another thing I've rarely done is rely on quotes. For example, I can do a phone interview with Sandy Koufax because I know him so well, or Steve Garvey. But if I don't know the athlete at all, if I'm going to do Dave Parker, I've got to go down and see him. When I do get down there, I don't just go down there to the locker room and ask him these incredibly brilliant and cute questions. What I used to do was sit in the locker room. If I wanted to do a story on Wills, I'd sit there and talk to Don Drysdale, maybe, or to the trainer. But I'd watch Wills, watch him when he came in and see everything he did. I feel you can learn an awful lot more by watching a guy, particularly when he doesn't know he's being observed.

You know, I have had athletes tell me they steer clear of me because "Murray will misquote you." I requested an interview with Gary Player one time and that message came back to me. I replied that I not only don't misquote 'em, I very rarely quote 'em. Which is true, unless a guy says something incredibly important.

Oh, I have made up quotes a couple of times, I'm not sure whether I did this or not — I get credit for it — but Arnold Palmer made a 12 on a hole and I don't know what he said when he came in but we made up a quote for him. Somebody said, "Well, Arnold, how did you make 12 on the hole?" And Arnold answered, "I missed a short putt for an 11."

Arnold never said that. But I think it's justified from time to time, making up a quote like that. If you need a last line for a column, it's great, it's wild.

QUESTION: Careful, you're unmasking yourself. Are you the Janet Cooke of sports columnists?

MURRAY: No, no. As a matter of fact, I wish I could make up quotes, but I'm not that clever. I just don't quote. Unless the guy's very fascinating, unless he's really got something to say, I just stand aside.

QUESTION: How do you maintain the balance between opinions and description?

MURRAY: There are times our profession requires you to be an opinionated jerk. And there are days when you don't have any opinion. If you have an opinion, for example, on the baseball strike, okay, you write an opinion column.

Anytime I want to attack something I would much rather do a satirical piece because in the first place it's unanswerable. Second place, you can get in very telling blows. But with satire you've got to be clever. You can't be heavy-handed with satire or it falls apart in your hands. I would rather not come out everyday with an opinion, would you?

QUESTION: No, I wouldn't. I don't have an opinion about things every day.

MURRAY: Ah, sure you do.

QUESTION: Well, not about what they let me write. I'm not allowed to write about Ronald Reagan.

MURRAY: Well, I don't mean political opinion. That's more for cartoonists. I'm talking about an opinion on, say, tampering with grades to get good athletes or the baseball strike. I think the public gets tired of a columnist being a common scold.

QUESTION: Yeah. But H.L. Mencken did it successfully. I've never been able to figure out what the hell his charm was, or why he was able to get away with his railings.

MURRAY: I've seen some things Mencken wrote. For their day I guess they were outrageous and daring.

As a matter of fact, I've had so many friends come up to me and tell me what a great writer this Russell Baker is. I've been struggling for years and half the time I don't know what the hell he's talking about.

QUESTION: I know. He's hard to understand.

MURRAY: He is. His humor is, you know, a very acquired taste. Like truffles, or something.

QUESTION: Name the columnists you admire greatly.

MURRAY: I admire Red Smith. Yeah, I like those elegant sentences he is able to write, his finely-tuned prose. You know, so many people come to me and put down Jimmy Breslin. I couldn't give a damn. I love to read Breslin, particularly when he gets into high dudgeon. I liked Jimmy Cannon. I like Breslin. Mel Durslag I think is a fine writer. Blackie Sherrod is good. So is Furman Bisher in Atlanta.

QUESTION: I've often heard Red Smith talk about leads, the importance of leads and leads he admires. Are there leads that stick in your mind?

MURRAY: Oh, yeah. The one lead I wrote one time is kind of an interesting story I always tell. I wrote a lead about Sonny Liston — I interviewed him some place, Chicago, I think it was — so I sat and watched this monster. And, I wrote a lead that read, "The first look you get at Sonny Liston you only hope it don't bite." Now, I marked the word don't "cq" three times, because I was trying to convey what a truck driver might say: "My God, I hope it don't bite." So before my book came out, I called them up and told them there were some places where the grammar was wrong, but I want it wrong because I'm doing it for effect. If you correct it, then it's got to come out, "The first look you get at Sonny Liston you only hope it does not bite." Or even, "It doesn't bite." And they don't convey the same, you know, as "My God, I hope it don't bite." And they all agreed, yes, they understood perfectly. So the damn book came out: "The first look you get at Sonny Liston you only hope it does not bite." I flung the thing into the air and thought, "Geez, the proofroom in the newspaper can get it right, you guys can't?"

If you have a great lead you can be home free. Like one time when Notre Dame got the hell kicked out of them by USC, my lead was, "Okay, who was the wise guy who ate meat on Friday?" The lead that sort of got me the job was, again, after USC had beaten Notre Dame. I said, "Crowd couldn't have been more shocked if the Christians ate the Lions." A good lead is very important. But I'll tell you what is more important to me — I'm sure to anybody — is a good idea.

QUESTION: Have you heard that story about the guy who was covering a big football game somewhere and he had to write a couple of stories and his column. A hooker gets into an elevator with him and says, "For a hundred dollars I'll do anything you want." And he said, "How about a lead, a sidebar and a column?" What have been the most exasperating things you've had to deal with since you've been writing a column?

MURRAY: Well, first it was, you know, the retina came loose on the left eye. It was operated on and apparently repaired. I went back to work and everything was fine. Then all of a sudden, I was watching television one night, and crash! It was just like the whole picture flowed onto the floor.

And then the doctors did all those operations. And they all failed. There were all kinds of complications in both eyes. There was a period there when I couldn't see to write or read. So I had to learn to dictate into a cassette. The Los Angeles Times was absolutely great to me, did everything they could to help me and keep me working. Dictating was rough. There's a big difference between talking and writing. It was traumatic, believe me.

QUESTION: How old are you?

MURRAY: I'm 61.

QUESTION: How much longer do you want to keep doing this? Four more years? Then move to Palm Springs?

MURRAY: Yeah, David, the only thing that bothers me is inflation. When I was in high school, more than 40 years ago, if somebody had said, "Sign this paper and you'll get $32.50 a week for the rest of your life," I would have signed it. That was good money in those days. Now, Jesus, steak will be $5,000 a pound soon.

Anyway, I don't want to hang on too long. I still want to be able to do it, have a good year, like Pete Rose. I don't want to embarrass myself. You know, at 88 writing about Ernie Nevers.

JIM MURRAY, syndicated sports columnist for the Los Angeles Times, was interviewed by David Israel, a general columnist for the Los Angeles Herald Examiner, on the ins and outs of writing a sports column. The article appeared in the November 1981 Bulletin.

He wrote the hell out of a sports column

Roger Kahn

Tomorrow Red Smith would reach the age of 74. He would be springy of step, ebullient with youth and well-tuned to a world that is newly born each day. Still, he would be 74 years old.

"When is your deadline?" Smith asked.

The day had broken a cool autumn blue. I mentioned a target date.

"Maybe you'd better hurry," Smith said. "My contract at The Times expires in five weeks and I haven't heard a word about renewal."

Paranoia is a classic affliction of writers. Somehow, you will not be allowed to finish a work in progress. If you do finish, a dozen critics will hurl typewriters at your head. Should the critics be kind, the public will ignore what you have written. "Hell," says one durable writer of my acquaintance, "I admit I'm paranoid, but what else can you be when they're persecuting you?"

One of Red Smith's charms, across the 30 years I've known him, has been an abiding, diffidently expressed confidence. Pressed once by an admirer who hailed him as a titan of the press box, Smith winced but then conceded, "I know I'm a pretty good speller." He has not seemed to perceive the world as freighted with enemies. Rather, his views of sport, prose and himself suggest that he is working for an audience of friends. The people he writes for are literate. They know which base is second. They delight in his stories, jests, insightful reporting.

"You aren't serious," I said. "Your column is the best thing in The Times sports section."

"You aren't the editor of The Times," Smith said.

The next day, as Smith entered his 75th year, I telephoned A.M. Rosenthal, a complex, gifted, unsentimental journalist who runs The Times.

"Not renew Red Smith's contract?" Rosenthal said softly, as though in shock. "His contract will never be over. Do you know what Red means to me? Personally? I get depressed sometimes editing this paper. But whenever I get down I say to myself, 'Wait a minute. I hired Red Smith.' "

The full name is Walter Wellesley Smith. The late Stanley Woodward, a sports editor of irresistible ferocity and brilliance, found a woman's school named Walter somewhere and thus could claim that Red was the only man in history "named after three girls' colleges." The claim goes undenied. Smith's style in writing and life is graceful and measured, sensible and joyous: culture without pomposity. He lost his first wife, Catherine, to cancer, and he himself underwent surgery two years ago for a dangerous growth deep in the gut. But he does not dwell on pain. I assume he can write a tortured sentence, but I cannot remember reading one.

At work, Smith avoids the terrible triad of sports journalism: shrillness (as in televised pro football), overstatement (as in Olympian battles under purple sunsets) and mindless emotionalism (as in the beatification of Thurman Munson). His eyes may mist, so to speak, for vanished friends, but he spares us shrieks, polemics and grunting sobs.

A specially choice sample of Smith's style described the balance of power between the late Walter O'Malley, czar of all the Dodgers, and Bowie Kuhn, a pleasant, somewhat stiff attorney who has found gainful employment as commissioner of baseball. "When O'Malley sends out for coffee," Smith wrote,"Bowie Kuhn asks, 'One lump or two?' " Writers 50 years Smith's junior had spent a thousand words making that point less well.

It is an error to perceive Smith's civilized approach as mild. We were discussing one sportswriter who is gifted but so painfully self-important that he recently remarked, "I have perfected the magazine sports profile."

"Did you read his latest piece?" I asked.

"No," Smith said. "I didn't have the energy."

Once, when people at Sports Illustrated were altering his stuff, Smith commented, "They put words into my copy that I've spent my life not using."

"Such as?" I asked.

"Such as 'moreover.' "

Boredom is the leopard that stalks the stag. Sports patterns repeat. Athletes say similar things from one decade to the next. Today's champion may not glitter like yesterday's hero whom we remember in the soft focus of our own youth. Not long ago someone asked Smith if he was beginning to find baseball dull after a lifetime in press boxes.

"Baseball," Smith said, "is dull only to dull minds."

By its terse eloquence, the comment leads one away from the

core of Smith's indomitable enthusiasm. The source is not base-ball, his favorite sport. We are considering a professional, not a fan. The source is the newspaper business. "I love the newspaper business," Smith says, "whether I'm writing sports or anything else."

Red and Phyllis Smith own a colonial home in the New York suburb of New Canaan, Conn., but they take special pleasure in the cedar house they have had built near a Vineyard crossroads known as Chilmark. The house is airy and modern, without being extreme. It is secluded, but in minutes the Smiths can drive to fishing boats that ride out through Menemsha Bite, or to a sandy spit that commands head-clearing views or to a promontory 142 steps above a sandy beach backed by cliffs of clay.

This windy day Smith looked ruddy rather than red. He describes himself as ill-coordinated and four-eyed. He also says that he is prolix and maundering. Actually, he is only one of the above (he does wear eyeglasses). He wore a blue sweater and gray slacks as he approached the arrival gate and his walk was quick. Though the red hair has gone white, his face retains a young expression, and a look that suggests he is about to smile.

At the cedar house, he set a fire within a white brick hearth. He has been trying not to smoke for several years but my pack weakened his resolve. His hands shook slightly as he lit up. "I attributed this to alcohol once," Smith said, "but there was a time when I couldn't drink a drop and the shaking persisted. Turns out it isn't whiskey, but senility."

He does not like to play the dean, much less the critic, but eventually he agreed to compare sports sections past and present. "There is truly a generally higher level of competence," he said, "than there was, say, 30 years ago. We had illiterates then who grew up from copyboy, if you'll pardon me."

I pardoned him. Thirty years ago at the New York Herald Tribune, I drew $26.50 a week putting away Red Smith's mail.

"Actually, there aren't as many papers," Smith said, "so there aren't as many jobs for bums. On the other hand there's a spreading tendency on newspapers to use a magazine approach. Newspaper editors are developing a notion that everybody has watched every event. I appreciate depth in coverage, but newspapers shouldn't abdicate who won and by what score.

"Then, even though the general level of competence is higher, I don't see anywhere a developing [Joe] Palmer,

[John] Lardner, [Westbrook] Pegler, [W. O.] McGeehan or [Frank] Graham."

It is hard to say exactly why. Television salaries attract some journalists before they learn really how to write. Educational standards have sagged and it is possible to win a journalism degree at certain universities without studying the American and English stylists who developed the written language. (Let alone Vergil or Aeschylus.) More people attend more schools. Each may learn less.

When Smith graduated from Notre Dame as a journalism major in 1927, he was equipped both with a sure sense of sports and a classical background. "The only team I tried out for was track," he said, "and that mostly as a way of avoiding gym. I couldn't run fast enough for the half mile so I thought perhaps I could run long enough for the mile, and I competed in a freshman-varsity handicap. Soon I was last, about 10 laps behind. Rockne coached track and he said, 'All right. You can drop out now.' So I not only finished last, I didn't finish."

We began to play a game of capsule columns. I'd mention a name and Smith would comment.

Sugar Ray Robinson: "At the St. Louis zoo in Forest Park, a black jaguar was the most beautiful thing I ever saw. I'd get in front of the cage some days and say, 'Good morning, Ray.' Robinson said I made him conceited when I wrote about him."

Frank Leahy: "I suppose he laid it on too thick. He made one of the seconding speeches for Eisenhower in 1956 and you thought he might really say, 'We've got to win this for the Gipper.' I took pleasure in needling him, but at the bottom Leahy was sincere. I believe Frank always stood up when his mother entered a room."

Muhammad Ali: "In 19 years, the act has never really changed. We've had telephone conversations where he's said, 'Do you have enough?' Whatever his positions, how can a guy in my business hate a subject that cooperative?"

George Steinbrenner: "When I was sick, I got a note from George saying we'd had differences, but he respected me. It was a lovely note, but George has gotten to be pretty impossible."

Eddie Arcaro: "He was the best at what he did, and he was always approachable, always candid. Most of the time that's true with the great champions."

Ernest Hemingway: "I didn't know him well, but I remember meeting him at Shor's and I said, 'Thank you for putting me in the book.' (Smith draws praise in *Across the River and into the*

Trees.) Later in Cuba Frank Graham and I were watching an auto race on the Malacon and afterwards he invited us to his house. In The New Yorker profile, he seems to be a drunken braggart, but I found him diffident, a little shy. He was a big gentle guy with what seemed a very sweet disposition. After he won the Nobel Prize, he was quoted as saying that he used the first $25,000 to get even. I had the bad taste to ask him why he was broke. 'What bothers me,' I said, 'is that with the exception of Edgar Guest, you are the best-selling author in America, and the top guy should be able to afford anything.'

"He said that with his first successful book [*The Sun Also Rises*], he gave the royalties to the mother of his son. With the next [*A Farewell to Arms*], he gave the royalties to his own mother.

"Then he said, 'Red, a fellow's only got so many books like that in him.' "

No less a weight than Gertrude Stein postulated that being an artist begins with recognizing one's limits. She said that when Picasso showed her his poetry. Smith does not compose sagas or novels, and his style shimmers, like a bark at sea, rather than shattering waters, like a Leviathan. Certain dogged plodders, confusing easy reading with easy writing, see Smith as an airy sort, more concerned with lightness of line than with depth of thought. But I know no one, Nobel laureates or Pulitzer poets, more serious about the craft of writing.

Smith came out of Green Bay, where his father ran a grocery, with ample native talent. His triumph is the way he developed the talent across five decades. He applied at The Times in 1927 but was turned down. He then worked at newspapers in Green Bay, St. Louis and Philadelphia, hoping somehow to make New York. When Stanley Woodward finally brought him to the Herald Tribune, it was 1945, 28 years after Smith's first newspaper job. His stuff had gotten better and better, but Woodward had to lie to Tribune brass about the new man's age. He shaved the honest total by five years.

The Tribune was getting what Casey Stengel so admired, "one of them men with experience." Smith could and did and does write the hell out of a sports column. He also knew how to cover a warehouse fire. No one was better prepared, or more anxious to play the Palace. His Tribune columns attracted a syndicate of 90 newspapers. Then, after the Tribune died, The Times hired Smith in 1971.

"The one trouble with him now," insists a younger writer,

who would be radical if he had the patience to read Karl Marx, "is that he doesn't challenge sport's fascistic values."

Ah, but Red challenges sham, pomposity, grandiloquence, self-righteousness and the self-anointed priesthood of the arrogant. I believe those qualities sum up a man like Mussolini.

Growing with each decade, Smith has lately become the most distinguished champion of the baseball players' union. That issue, the players' right to share the giant jackpot, is as political as sports really gets these days. For all its commercialism, sports is not a political system but an art form. An American art form. "Slot 44" is neither fascist nor communist: It is a way of making several yards. Sparky Anderson, who barred facial hair in Cincinnati, was not attacking the New Left. He wanted Bench and Rose and Morgan to look well-groomed. Smith does not confuse the demands of a head counselor with the fiats of a dictator. He is alert to real issues, such as players' rights, without finding sociology in a line drive.

He describes Chris Evert Lloyd and Jimmy Connors as they are (self-occupied is what they are, before anything else). He does not constantly try, as Hemingway said of Jimmy Cannon, to write columns that "leave the English language for dead." His only demand is that the reader be able to think, which is probably the first demand he found at Notre Dame when he arrived there 55 years ago.

Newspaper libraries show no specific predecessor. Oh, Heywood Broun was literate and Pegler was irreverent, but both went global. Current sports pages are blank of an inheritor. Once I asked Smith if he had any superstitions and he said immediately, "Only the Holy Roman Church." Seeking the source of such a response is as fruitless as analyzing laughter. You had better simply rejoice that the phrase is there.

One does not say that directly to Mr. Smith. He has lived a long time — he is twice a great-grandfather — but, outbursts of praise make him uncomfortable.

Crisp Vineyard night was lowering on the cedar house. It was time, we all agreed, to open a bottle of wine.

ROGER KAHN, writer for The New Yorker and author of The Boys of Summer *and other books, interviewed Red Smith for Notre Dame Magazine. The article was reprinted in the November 1980 Bulletin. Smith died January 15, 1982.*

Writings on writing

Which books should every newsroom have?

Don Murray

Books on writing — and manuals on sex — can be helpful, but they are no substitute for the act itself.

The newspaper that wants to improve writing will first of all have to allow writers to write. This means bringing writers into the assignment process, encouraging discussion of different approaches to stories, stimulating experiments in style and form, encouraging revision and rewarding writing that works. It also means accepting failure as an essential part of the writing process. Most newspapers are poorly written because there are no significant or interesting failures — just dull, bland competence.

The text for improving writing is made up of the best stories being published in the paper. These stories deserve special attention. They should be reprinted and passed around, posted and discussed. What made them good? What would make them better?

Such positive reinforcement is alien to most city rooms. Writers and editors exist in an adversary relationship. The editor tells the writer what to do, and when the writer does it the editor tells the writer what was wrong with it. Attack leads to counterattack. The emphasis is on the weakest stories, the most obvious errors, the poorest writers.

The newspaper that wants to improve writing has to respond to the best writing it's publishing. And then once that writing is identified, the paper should encourage the writers and editors who have produced it to work together to improve the level of writing and to share what they are learning in the process. At The Boston Globe I published interviews with some of the best writers and editors who were willing to share their experience and their craft. At the Providence Journal-Bulletin, Christopher Scanlan and I are getting writers and editors to write and share accounts of the making of good stories under such titles as, "How I got the story," "How I wrote the story," "How I edited the story." Accounts such as these encourage writers and editors to learn what they did instinctively when the work went well and allows them to share their knowledge with their colleagues.

Once the city room develops an evolving test of good writing then some other books can stimulate and support this activity. Some of my favorites are:

General books on writing

On Writing Well: An Informal Guide to Writing Nonfiction, 2nd edition, William Zinsser, Harper & Row (1980, NYC, 187 pp). In my opinion, this is the single best book on writing available today. Zinsser was one of the stars of the New York Herald Tribune, was a columnist for Life and The New York Times, is the author of nine books, was a teacher of writing at Yale and is now executive editor of the Book-of-the-Month Club. He practices what he preaches.

I remember when this book first came out. I picked it up on my way to a flight from Boston to San Francisco and read it from first page to last at a sitting. Since then I've reread it, taught it and had it distributed in city rooms. If I were an editor, I'd buy a pile of Zinssers, put them on the corner of my desk and hope they'd get stolen.

There are a number of other books in this category. The best-known, of course, is *The Elements of Style,* William Strunk Jr., with revisions, an introduction and a chapter on writing by E. B. White, 3rd edition, Macmillan (1979, NYC, 85 pp). White's comments on writing are brilliant, but they are limited in scope, and much of the book involves stylistic rules that are sometimes eccentric and sometimes trivial. It should be on every writer's shelf, but it is an uneven book, and I don't think it comes close to Zinsser.

Interviews with writers

I have three shelves of books in my office that are collections of interviews with writers. These books record a kind of shop-talk that can be inspiring. It allows the writers on the paper to share writing problems and solutions with the best writers of our time. The best of these books is the series called, *Writers At Work — The Paris Review Interviews.* There are now five of these collections, all in print in Penguin Paperback. The list of those interviewed is too long to reproduce, but imagine having the opportunity to talk shop with such writers as William Faulkner, Frank O'Connor, Robert Penn Warren, Truman Capote, Robert Frost, Marianne Moore, T. S. Eliot, Ernest Hemingway, Mary McCarthy, Ralph Ellison, Norman Mailer, Lillian Hellman, John Updike, John Cheever, Joan Didion and many, many more.

These interviews have been carefully constructed, often revised and edited with the assistance of the writer. They are published with an example of a manuscript page and a brief biography, often describing the places and the conditions where the writers work. I have collected more than 8,000 quotes from writers that I have in 24 three-inch thick looseleaf binders, but a high percentage of my best quotes comes from these five volumes. Anyone serious about writing should have these books near his or her writing desk.

Collections of good writing

There are now three volumes of *Best Newspaper Writing,* each edited by Roy Peter Clark and published by the Modern Media Institute, 556 Central Avenue, St. Petersburg, Florida, 33701. These volumes reprint the stories that won the ASNE writing competition in 1979, 1980 and 1981. The stories are published with interviews Clark has conducted with the writers. I think these stories and interviews should be in every city room. No matter if some of the choices make people mad; they are a point of argument, a place to begin discussion of what is good newspaper writing today.

I'd also have some paperback copies of *A Treasury of Great Reporting* available in the city room. It is edited by Louis L. Snyder and Richard B. Morris, and published by Pocket Books. This collection goes back hundreds of years and puts newspaper writing in a historical context. The examples of good writing in this book show that good writing is good writing, no matter the time, place or style. Many of these stories stimulate and inspire.

There are also anthologies of work by individual writers that should be shared in newsrooms where writing is respected. My favorites, in order, are:

The McPhee Reader, edited by William L. Howarth, Vintage Paperback (1977, NYC, 385 pp). This is a fine introduction to a writer that many people consider the best nonfiction writer publishing today. The introduction to the reader by Howarth provides a fascinating description of McPhee's writing methods. The way in which he is able to write, and the length at which The New Yorker allows him to write, will not translate into city room practice, but he establishes a standard, an approach and a voice with which all journalists should be familiar. All of McPhee's books are now in print, and all can be read with profit.

Essays of E. B. White, Harper & Row (1977, NYC, 277 pp). Every writer should be familiar with the style of the old master. Any of his books of essays will instruct the beginning nonfiction writer.

The Orwell Reader: Fiction, Essays and Reportage, Harvest Paperback (1961, NYC, 222 pp). Every serious journalist should return to George Orwell on a regular basis. All of his journalism is now printed in a series of paperbacks. His essay, "Politics and the English Language," should be required reading for every political reporter once a year.

Reporting, by Lillian Ross, Dodd, Mead Paperback (1981, NYC, 442 pp). This classic of reporting and writing has just been reissued with a valuable introduction by the author.

Poison Penmanship, The Gentle Art of Muckraking, by Jessica Mitford, Vintage Paperback (1980, NYC, 277 pp). This book not only includes examples of her work, but an introduction and a running, witty, bitey commentary by the author.

There are hundreds of books in print that show the range of good nonfiction writing. They demonstrate the vitality of this genre. Although fiction, poetry and drama are what is taught in English literature classes, some of us, at least, believe that nonfiction writing in the second half of the 20th century may be the genre for which our time will be remembered. It would be easy to list a hundred books that could be read with profit by working nonfiction writers, but such a list should come from the writers and editors in a particular city room. A book budget that would allow a lending library of books that people on the paper could recommend, borrow and share would be an excellent investment.

I would also include books of fiction, poetry and drama. The lines between the different forms of writing increasingly blur, and they should. This doesn't mean that reporters should make up facts: It does mean that the techniques of language and structure can be used by writers who are building literature from facts.

Textbooks

News Reporting and Writing, 2nd Edition, by Melvin Mencher, William C. Brown (1981, Dubuque, Iowa, 634 pp), is a textbook for journalism students from which experienced journalists can learn. It is also a textbook that demonstrates good writing as well as argues for it.

Is this list eccentric and personal? I certainly hope so. But these are books from which I continue to learn, they are books I read and reread and they are books I would seed in city rooms across the country. And what about the other books that editors and writers on the paper prefer? Buy them. Get them in circulation. If you spread these books around and develop that primary text from the paper's own best writing — together with accounts about how it got made, was reported, written and edited — then enthusiasm for writing may become contagious in the city room.

John B. Bremner

If someone somewhere is offering an award for benign importunity, I'll nominate Loren Ghiglione, editorial board chairman of The Bulletin. Only yesterday, it seems, he asked me for this piece: deadline tomorrow. Make the list as long or as short as you like, he said.

I prefer the short list requested annually by student editors: "If you were going to be stranded on a desert island and could take only three books, which would you take?" This kind of footnote occasionally accompanies the request: "Don't include the Bible. Lest they be deemed irreligious, most Crusoes include the Bible, whether they want it or not."

My list of three last year comprised: *The Complete Works of William Shakespeare, The American Heritage Dictionary of the English Language* and Dale Carnegie's *How to Make Friends and Influence People*. I should have copied Chesterton and named only one: *Shipbuilding for Amateurs*.

For a really long list, see Warren C. Price, *The Literature of Journalism: An Annotated Bibliography* (Minneapolis: University of Minnesota Press, 1959), and its sequel, Warren C. Price and Calder M. Pickett, *An Annotated Journalism Bibliography: 1959-1968* (Minneapolis: University of Minnesota Press, 1970). We await a third volume.

But Mr. Ghiglione prefers a list of 20-30 books "about good writing and editing." All right, Mr. Legree, here's a list:

Dictionaries

Webster's New International Dictionary, 2nd ed. Springfield, Mass.: G. & C. Merriam, 1959. (That's Webster's *Second,* not Third. For a piercing essay on the difference, see Dwight Macdonald's "The String Untuned" in The New Yorker, March 10, 1962.)

William Morris, ed., *The American Heritage Dictionary of the English Language.* New York: American Heritage and Houghton Mifflin, 1969. (Probably the best of the abridged. Its several hundred usage notes are handy guides to effective writing. Excellent treatment of etymology.)

Geoffrey Payton, ed., *The Merriam-Webster Pocket Dictionary of Proper Names.* New York: Pocket Books, 1972. (Indispensable on a copydesk. Neither a dictionary of potted biographies nor a gazetteer, it guides copy editors through the barrage of proper names with which a desk is daily bombarded. Next to a regular dictionary, it is my most valuable reference.)

Tom Burnam, *The Dictionary of Misinformation.* New York: Ballantine Books, 1975. (What you know that just ain't so.)

Eric Partridge, *A Dictionary of Slang and Unconventional English,* 7th ed. New York: Macmillan, 1970. (The standard reference work on slang. Two volumes in one: 1,528 pages.)

William Morris and Mary Morris, *Morris Dictionary of Word and Phrase Origins.* New York: Harper & Row, 1977. (Thousands of word histories based upon sound research and written in lively style.)

Anthologies

Calder M. Pickett, *Voices of the Past.* Columbus, Ohio: Grid, 1977. (Probably the best anthology of key documents in the history of American journalism, collected by probably the best historian of American journalism.)

Louis L. Snyder and Richard B. Morris, eds., *A Treasury of Great Reporting,* rev. ed. New York: Simon and Schuster, 1962. (Still an invaluable, instructive collection.)

John Hohenberg, ed., *The Pulitzer Prize Story.* New York: Columbia University Press, 1959. (Administrator of the Pulitzer Prizes from 1954 to 1976, Hohenberg chooses and comments on some of the best of the winners from 1917 to 1958.)

John Hohenberg, ed., *The Pulitzer Prize Story II.* New York: Columbia University Press, 1980. (Hohenberg brings the Pulitzer story up to date — well, almost; the 1981 story should be a lulu.)

Writing & usage

H.W. Fowler, *A Dictionary of Modern English Usage,* 2nd ed., New York: Oxford University Press, 1965. (The bible.)

Theodore M. Bernstein, *Watch Your Language.* Great Neck, N.Y.: Channel Press, 1958. (One of the earliest and best of the former wordsmith of The New York Times.)

Theodore M. Bernstein, *The Careful Writer.* New York: Atheneum, 1965. (Probably the master's best.)

Jacques Barzun, *Simple & Direct.* New York: Harper & Row, 1975. (An introduction to the art of becoming self-conscious and analytic about words; a rhetoric for writers, in the strict sense of *rhetoric.*)

William Strunk Jr. and E. B. White, *The Elements of Style,* 3rd ed. New York: Macmillan, 1979. (Clear, brief, bold. Student White has made Professor Strunk's "little book" a magnum opus.)

Bergen Evans and Cornelia Evans, *A Dictionary of Contemporary American Usage.* New York: Random House, 1957. (Still contemporary.)

William Morris and Mary Morris, *Harper Dictionary of Contemporary Usage.* New York: Harper & Row, 1975. (Enriched by the comments of its 136 consultants on usage.)

Harry G. Nickles, *The Dictionary of Do's and Don'ts.* New York: McGraw-Hill, 1974. (A delightful devastation of cliches.)

William Zinsser, *On Writing Well.* New York: Harper & Row, 1976. (Ably dedicated to the proposition that the language of good journalism is good English.)

John Moore, *You English Words.* London: Collins, 1961. (A beautiful view of the language from its birthplace.)

John B. Bremner, *Words on Words: A Dictionary for Writers and Others Who Care About Words.* New York: Columbia University Press, 1980. (His wife likes it. His students have to read it.)

Texts

John Hohenberg, *The Professional Journalist,* 4th ed. New York: Holt, Rinehart and Winston, 1978. (Probably the best among several good texts on reporting.)

Alfred A. Crowell, *Creative News Editing,* 2nd ed. Dubuque, Iowa: Wm. C. Brown, 1975. (Probably the best among several good texts on copy editing.)

John B. Bremner, *HTK: A Study in News Headlines.* Topeka, Kan.: Palindrome Press, Mainline Printing, 1975. (Needs to be brought up to date because of downstyle and horizontal trends, but its principles of good headline writing remain sound.)

John B. Opdycke, *Harper's English Grammar*. New York: Harper & Row, 1966. (An authoritative, comprehensive work on grammar.)

Maxwell Nurnberg, *Punctuation Pointers*. New York: Scholastic Book Services, 1968. (This may be out-of-print, but try to dig up a copy. It's a simple, tight, clear explanation of punctuation principles.)

Other

Eugene J. McCarthy and James J. Kilpatrick, with illustrations by Jeff MacNelly, *A Political Bestiary*. New York: McGraw-Hill, 1978. (Oxymoronically born of the truism that the proper study of mankind is animals, this brilliant satire should be required reading for all who would strive to translate governmental gobbledygook.)

Afferbeck Lauder, *Let Stalk Strine*. Sydney: Ure Smith, 1965. (No one from up over should venture down under without this lexicon. You don't have to read the entries in afferbeck lauder. For the price of the book, ask Emma Chisit.)

That's 28. Add the *AP-UPI Stylebook* and *The World Almanac* and you have your 30, Mr. Chairman. Comes now the time for mine.

Roy Peter Clark

George Orwell, "Politics and the English Language," from *Shooting an Elephant and Other Essays* (Harcourt Brace Jovanovich, Inc., 1950). This essay should be nailed to each journalist's desk. Good advice for writers. Shows relationship between language abuse and political abuse. I recommend all of Orwell's nonfiction.

William Strunk Jr. and E. B. White, *The Elements of Style,* third edition (Macmillan, 1979). A classic. Usually used by beginners, but more valuable for experienced writers.

William Zinsser, *On Writing Well* (Harper & Row, 1976). A narrative Strunk & White. Practical. Fun to read. This book can really turn someone's writing around. Especially valuable in its discussion of "clutter."

Donald Murray, *A Writer Teaches Writing* (Houghton Mifflin, 1968). One of the most important teachers of writing in the country explains the process of writing. Important for writers and teachers (editors).

The Riverside Shakespeare (Houghton Mifflin, 1974). It never hurts to have ol' Willie lyin' around.

The King James Bible. A great bargain. Will make you both a better person and a better writer.

The Compact Edition of the Oxford English Dictionary, ed. James A.H. Murray and others. Two volumes in microprint. Available from book clubs at great discount. This is the most important source on language ever compiled. And in this edition it has become widely available. It has been brought up to date by *A Supplement to the OED,* ed. R.W. Burchfield (Oxford: Clarendon Press, 1972).

The American Heritage Dictionary, ed. William Morris (Houghton Mifflin, 1973). A wonderful, interesting dictionary, especially for journalists. Its Usage Panel discusses questions of usage. A compromise between the descriptive and prescriptive schools of lexicography.

Donald Hall, *Writing Well* (Little Brown, 1976). An advanced college text. But contains excellent advice on writing for everyone. Hall practices what he preaches.

H.W. Fowler, *Modern English Usage* (Oxford University Press, 1975). If you groove on the subjunctive or nonrestrictive clauses, this cranky classic is for you.

Joan Didion, *Slouching Towards Bethlehem* (Simon and Schuster, 1968). One of the purest, most elegant writing styles in America.

Peter Elbow, *Writing Without Teachers* (Oxford University Press, 1973). A wild, inventive, idiosyncratic approach to writing. Contains many exciting ideas about the writing process.

The John McPhee Reader, ed. William L. Howarth (Vintage Books, 1976). Excerpts from one of America's great journalists. An interesting foreword describes McPhee's working method.

"Adam Smith," *The Money Game* (Random House, 1968). Proves that writing about business and finance can be fun — for the reader.

Nora Ephron, *Crazy Salad* (Bantam Books, 1976) and *Scribble Scribble* (Bantam Books, 1978). Ephron is a strong reporter and a clever writer.

Essays of E. B. White (Harper Colophon, 1977). As valuable as Strunk and White.

Melvin Mencher, *News Reporting and Writing* (Wm. C. Brown, 1977). The best college text on reporting. A thorough introduction to the craft of journalism.

Ronald Weber, ed., *The Reporter As Artist: A Look at the New Journalism Controversy* (Hastings House, 1974). Essays examining all aspects of the so-called New Journalism. Anticipates some of the issues raised in recent Pulitzer controversies.

John B. Bremner, *Words on Words: A Dictionary for Writers and Others Who Care About Words* (Columbia University Press, 1980). Excellent for writers or copy editors.

Willard R. Espy, *Words at Play* (Clarkson N. Potter, 1975). Will convince anyone that creativity with language can be fun.

Denis Brian, *Murderers and Other Friendly People* (McGraw, 1973). A fine book on the art of interviewing.

Donald Murray, *The Newswriter's Craft* (The Boston Globe Pequot Press Inc.). A collection of material produced while Murray was writing coach of The Boston Globe. Some of the best advice for writers I've ever seen.

Rene J. Cappon, *The Word* (working title), a supplement to the AP Stylebook. One of the AP's top editors gives advice on writing and usage. May be ready for publication in 1982.

Roy Peter Clark, ed., *Best Newspaper Writing 1981* (Modern Media Institute, 556 Central Avenue, St. Petersburg, Fla. 33701). Contains most recent winners of ASNE Distinguished Writing Awards. Features, news, sports, commentary. Interviews with writers.

For its September 1981 issue, The Bulletin asked three writing coaches to list books on writing and editing that every newsroom should own. Offering their opinions were: DONALD MURRAY, a Pulitzer Prize-winning editorial writer for The Boston Herald, who now serves as a professor of English at the University of New Hampshire; JOHN BREMNER, a professor at the University of Kansas, and ROY PETER CLARK, who organizes and directs writing seminars for the Modern Media Institute.

Acknowledgments

The articles reprinted in this book appeared first in The Bulletin, the magazine of the American Society of Newspaper Editors.

The book draws most heavily from special reports produced in the last two years by seven members of the magazine's editorial board: Dave Burgin, editor, Orlando Sentinel Star; Mary Anne Dolan, editor, Los Angeles Herald Examiner; James P. Gannon, executive editor, Des Moines Register and Tribune; Arthur Gelb, deputy managing editor, The New York Times; Frederick W. Hartmann, managing editor, The Florida Times-Union, Jacksonville; David Lawrence Jr., executive editor, Detroit Free Press; Jean Sharley Taylor, associate editor, Los Angeles Times.

The book's illustrations are the work of Richard Mayer, art director of the Detroit Free Press. Billie Keirstead, assistant director of the Modern Media Institute, offered guidance in the book's design, production and promotion. Gene Giancarlo, managing editor of The Bulletin, made sure the book was completed on budget; the Modern Media Institute, the ASNE Foundation and the 1981 ASNE board of directors, Michael J. O'Neill, president, made sure there was a budget to meet.

Finally, I confess to deciding which of many fine Bulletin articles on writing would be reprinted here. Those who do not agree with my choices may take solace in the definition of an editor — one who separates the wheat from the chaff and prints the chaff.

Loren Ghiglione